German
phrase book

✔ KU-545-666

AA Publishing

Contents

English edition prepared by First Edition Translations Ltd, Great Britain

Designed and produced by AA Publishing

Distributed in the United Kingdom by AA Publishing, Millstream, Maidenhead Road, Windsor, Berkshire SL4 5GD

First published in 1993 as Wat & Hoe Duits, © Uitgeverij Kosmos bv - Utrecht/Antwerpen

Van Dale Lexicografie bv - Utrecht/Antwerpen

This edition © Automobile Association Developments Limited 1999
Reprinted 2002
Reprinted 2003

A CIP catalogue record for this book is available from the British Library

ISBN: 0 7495 2137 6

Published by AA Publishing (a trading name of Automobile Association Developments Limited, whose registered office is Millstream, Maidenhead Road, Windsor, Berkshire SL4 5GD. Registered number 1878835).

A01577

Typeset by Anton Graphics Ltd, Andover, Hampshire

Printed & bound by G. Canale & C., Turin, Italy

Cover photograph: Altes Rathaus, Munich, AA Photo Library (T. Souter)

Find out more about AA Publishing and the wide range of services the AA provides by visiting our website at www.theAA.com

Introduction

● **Welcome to the AA's new Essential Phrase Books series, covering the most popular European languages and containing everything you'd expect from a comprehensive language series. They're concise, accessible and easy to understand, and you'll find them indispensable on your trip abroad.**

Each guide is divided into 15 themed sections and starts with a pronunciation table which explains the phonetic pronunciation to all the words and phrases you'll need to know for your trip, while at the back of the book is an extensive word list and grammar guide which will help you construct basic sentences in your chosen language.

Throughout the book you'll come across coloured boxes with a 🔊 beside them. These are designed to help you if you can't understand what your listener is saying to you. Hand the book over to them and encourage them to point to the appropriate answer to the question you are asking.

Other coloured boxes in the book - this time without the symbol - give alphabetical listings of themed words with their English translations beside them.

For extra clarity, we have put all English words and phrases in black, foreign language terms in red and their phonetic pronunciation in italic.

This phrase book covers all subjects you are likely to come across during the course of your visit, from reserving a room for the night to ordering food and drink at a restaurant and what to do if your car breaks down or you lose your traveller's cheques and money. With over 2,000 commonly used words and essential phrases at your fingertips you can rest assured that you will be able to get by in all situations, so let the Essential Phrase Book become your passport to a secure and enjoyable trip!

Pronunciation guide

The pronunciation provided should be read as if it were English, bearing in mind the following main points:

Vowels

a	is like **ar**	*ar*	as in **Kater**	*karter*
	or the **u** in cup	*u*	as in **Tasse**	*tusser*
ä	is like **ay** in may	*ay*	as in **spät**	*shpayt*
	or **e** in edible	*e*	as in **hält**	*helt*
e	is like **ay** in may	*ay*	as in **Nebel**	*naybel*
	or **e** in edible	*e*	as in **Mensch**	*mensh*
	or **air** in fair	*air*	as in **Schmerz**	*shmairts*
i	is like **i** in lick	*i*	as in **Mitte**	*mitter*
o	is like **oa** in boat	*oa*	as in **Motor**	*moator*
	or **o** in lock	*o*	as in **Socke**	*zokker*
ö	is like **u** in fur	*oe*	as in **öffnen**	*oefnen*
u	is like **oo** in ooze	*oo*	as in **Kur**	*koor*
ü	is like **ue** in cue	*ue*	as in **fünf**	*fuenf*

Consonants

Consonants are mainly as in English except for

g	like **g** in great	*g*	as in **Gigant**	*gigant*
j	like **y** in yes	*y*	as in **ja**	*yar*
s	when at beginning of word, like **z**	*z*	as in **Seife**	*zaifer*
v	like **f** in fish	*f*	as in **Volk**	*folk*
w	like **v** in vole	*v*	as in **Wagen**	*vargen*
z	like **ts** in cats	*ts*	as in **zwölf**	*tsvoelf*

At the end of a word **b**, **d**, and **g** change in sound to **p**, **t** and **k** respectively. The symbol **ß** (es-tset) stands for **ss** and is rare.

Some combinations of letters

au is pronounced *ow* as in cow; **eu** and **äu** are pronounced *oy* as in boy; **ie** is pronounced *ee* as in feet; **ei** and **ai** are pronounced as *ai* in Thai; **ch** is like **ch** in loch but rendered in the pronunciation as *kh*; **qu** is pronounced *kv*; **sp** and **st** at the start of a word are pronounced *shp* and *sht*; **sch** is also pronounced *sh*.

Stress

Usually on the leading syllable or on the stem (root) of the word, e.g. **stehen** (to stand) is stressed *shtay*en, **verstehen** (to understand) is stressed fair*shtay*en.

Useful lists

Useful lists

1.1 **T**oday or tomorrow?

What day is it today? _____	Welcher Tag ist heute?
	velkher tark ist hoyter?
Today's Monday_____	Heute ist Montag
	hoyter ist moantark
– Tuesday_____	Heute ist Dienstag
	hoyter ist deenstark
– Wednesday _____	Heute ist Mittwoch
	hoyter ist mittvokh
– Thursday_____	Heute ist Donnerstag
	hoyter ist donnerstark
– Friday_____	Heute ist Freitag
	hoyter ist fraitark
– Saturday _____	Heute ist Samstag/Sonnabend (S. Germany/ N. Germany)
	hoyter ist zamstark/zonnarbent
– Sunday _____	Heute ist Sonntag
	hoyter ist zonntark
in January _____	im Januar
	im yannooar
since February _____	seit Februar
	zait frebrooar
in spring_____	im Frühling
	im fruehling
in summer_____	im Sommer
	im zommer
in autumn _____	im Herbst
	im hairpst
in winter_____	im Winter
	im vinter
1997_____	neunzehnhundertsiebenundneunzig
	noyntsayn hoondert zeeben oont noyntsikh
the twentieth century ____	das zwanzigste Jahrhundert
	dass tsvantsikhster yarhoondert
What's the date today? ___	Der wievielte ist heute?
	dayr veefeelter ist hoyter?
Today's the 24th_____	Heute ist der vierundzwanzigste
	hoyter ist dayr fear oont tsvantsikhster
Monday 3 November _____ 1998	Montag, der 3 November 1998
	moantark dayr dritter november noyntsayn hoondert akht oont noyntsikh
in the morning _____	morgens
	morgens
midday _____	mittags (from about 11.30 - 2.00 p.m.)
	mittarks
in the afternoon_____	nachmittags
	nakhmittarks
in the evening _____	abends
	arbents
at night_____	nachts
	nakhts
this morning_____	heute morgen
	hoyter morgen

8

this afternoon _____	heute mittag
	hoyter mittark
this evening _____	heute nachmittag
	hoyter nakhmittark
tonight _____	heute abend
	hoyter arbent
last night _____	letzte nacht
	letster nakht
this week _____	diese Woche
	deezer vokher
next month _____	nächsten Monat
	nexten moanart
last year _____	voriges Jahr
	forigez yar
next... _____	nächste(n)/nächstes...
	nexter(n)/nextes
in...days/weeks/ _____	in ... Tagen/Wochen/Monaten/Jahren
months/years	*in ... targen/vokhen/moanarten/yaren*
...weeks ago _____	vor ... Wochen
	for ... vokhen
day off _____	der freie Tag
	dayr fraier tark

1 .2 Bank holidays

● **The most important** bank holidays in Germany are the following:

January 1	New Year's Day (Neujahr)
January 6	Epiphany (Hl. Drei Könige)
March/April	Good Friday, Easter and Easter Monday (Karfreitag, Ostersonntag und Ostermontag
May 1	May Day (Maifeiertag)
May	Ascension Day (Christi Himmelfahrt)
May/June	Whit Sunday and Whit Monday (Pfingstsonntag und Pfingstmontag)
*June	Corpus Christi (Fronleichnam)
*August 15	Feast of the Assumption (Mariä Himmelfahrt)
October 3	Day of German Unity (Tag der deutschen Einheit)
*November 1	All Saint's Day (Allerheiligen)
*November (Wed, variable)	Buss- und Bettag (day to repent and pray)
December 25/26	Christmas (Weihnachten)

Most shops, banks and government institutions are closed on these days. The dates marked with an asterisk are Catholic holidays and are mainly celebrated in the south of Germany. On Christmas Eve banks and shops tend to be closed in the afternoon.

Useful lists

1.3 What time is it?

What time is it? _____	Wie spät ist es?
	vee shpayt ist ez?
It's nine o'clock _____	Es ist neun Uhr
	ez ist noyn oòer
– five past ten _____	Es ist fünf nach zehn
	ez ist fuenf nakh tsayn
– a quarter past eleven ____	Es ist Viertel nach elf
	ez ist feartel nakh elf
– twenty past twelve_____	Es ist zehn nach zwölf
	ez ist tsayn nakh tsvoelf
– half past one _____	Es ist halb zwei
	ez ist halp tsvai
– twenty–five to three_____	Es ist fünf nach halb drei
	ez ist fuenf nakh halp drai
– a quarter to four_____	Es ist Viertel vor vier
	ez ist feartel for fear
– ten to five _____	Es ist zehn vor fünf
	ez ist tsayn for fuenf
– twelve noon_____	Es ist zwölf
	ez ist tsvoelf
– midnight_____	Es ist Mitternacht
	ez ist mitternakht
half an hour _____	eine halbe Stunde
	ainer halber shtoonder
What time? _____	Um wieviel Uhr?
	oom veefeel ooer?
What time can I come ____ round?	Wann kann ich vorbeikommen?
	vann kann ikh for bai kommen?
At..._____	Um...*oom...*
After..._____	Nach...*nakh...*
Before..._____	Vor...*for...*
Between...and..._____	Zwischen... und...
	tsvishen ... oont...
From...to..._____	Von ... bis...
	fon ... biss...
In...minutes _____	In ... Minuten
	in ... meenooten
– an hour _____	In einer Stunde
	in ainer shtoonder
– ...hours _____	In... Stunden
	In... shtoonden
– a quarter of an hour ____	In einer Viertelstunde
	in ainer feartel shtoonder
– three quarters of_____ an hour	In einer Dreiviertelstunde
	in ainer drai feartel shtoonder
early/late _____	zu früh/spät
	tsoo frue/shpayt
on time_____	rechtzeitig
	rekht tsaitikh
summertime _____	(die) Sommerzeit
	(dee) zommer tsait
wintertime _____	(die) Winterzeit
	(dee) vinter tsait

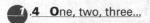

Useful lists

0	null	*nooll*
1	eins	*ains*
2	zwei	*tsvai*
3	drei	*drai*
4	vier	*fear*
5	fünf	*fuenf*
6	sechs	*zekhs*
7	sieben	*zeeben*
8	acht	*akht*
9	neun	*noyn*
10	zehn	*tsayn*
11	elf	*elf*
12	zwölf	*tsvoelf*
13	dreizehn	*draitsayn*
14	vierzehn	*feartsayn*
15	fünfzehn	*fuenftsayn*
16	sechzehn	*zekhtsayn*
17	siebzehn	*zeeptsayn*
18	achtzehn	*akht-tsayn*
19	neunzehn	*noyntsayn*
20	zwanzig	*tsvantsikh*
21	einundzwanzig	*ain oont tsvantsikh*
22	zweiundzwanzig	*tsvai oont tsvantsikh*
30	dreissig	*draissikh*
31	einunddreissig	*ain oont draissikh*
32	zweiunddreissig	*tsvai oont draissikh*
40	vierzig	*feartsikh*
50	fünfzig	*fuenftsikh*
60	sechzig	*zekhtsikh*
70	siebzig	*zeeptsikh*
80	achtzig	*akhttsikh*
90	neunzig	*noyntsikh*
100	hundert	*hoondert*
101	hunderteins	*hoondert ains*
110	hundertzehn	*hoondert tsayn*
120	hundertzwanzig	*hoondert tsvantsikh*
200	zweihundert	*tsvai hoondert*
300	dreihundert	*drai hoondert*
400	vierhundert	*fear hoondert*
500	fünfhundert	*fuenf hoondert*
600	sechshundert	*zekhs hoondert*
700	siebenhundert	*zeeben hoondert*
800	achthundert	*akht hoondert*
900	neunhundert	*noyn hoondert*
1,000	tausend	*towzent*
1,100	tausendeinhundert	*towzent ain hoondert*
2,000	zweitausend	*tsvai towzent*
10,000	zehntausend	*tsayn towzent*
100,000	hunderttausend	*hoondert towzent*
1,000,000	eine Million	*ainer millioan*

Useful lists

1st _____	erste *erster*
2nd _____	zweite *tsvaiter*
3rd _____	dritte *dritter*
4th _____	vierte *fearter*
5th _____	fünfte *fuenfter*
6th _____	sechste *zekhster*
7th _____	sieb(en)te *zeeb(en)ter*
8th _____	achte *akhter*
9th _____	neunte *noynter*
10th _____	zehnte *tsaynter*
11th _____	elfte *elfter*
12th _____	zwölfte *tsvoelfter*
13th _____	dreizehnter *draitsaynter*
14th _____	vierzehnte *feartsaynter*
15th _____	fünfzehnte *fuenftsaynter*
16th _____	sechzehnte *zekhtsaynter*
17th _____	siebzehnte *zeeptsaynter*
18th _____	achtzehnte *akht-tsaynter*
19th _____	neunzehnte *noyntsaynter*
20th _____	zwanzigste *tsvantsikhster*
21st _____	einundzwanzigste *ain oont tsvantsikhster*
22nd _____	zweiundzwanzigste *tsvai oont tsvantsikhster*
30th _____	dreissigste *draissikhster*
100th _____	hundertste *hoondertster*
1,000th _____	tausendste *towzentster*
once _____	einmal *ainmarl*
twice _____	zweimal *tsvaimarl*
double _____	das Doppelte *dass doppelter*
triple _____	das Dreifache *dass draifakher*
half _____	die Hälfte *dee haelfter*
a quarter _____	ein Viertel *ain feartel*
a third _____	ein Drittel *ain dritel*
a couple, a few, some ____	ein paar, einige, mehrere *ain par, ainiger, mayrerer*
2+4=6 _____	zwei und vier ist sechs *tsvai oont fear ist zekhs*
4-2=2 _____	vier weniger zwei ist zwei *fear vayniger tsvai ist tsvai*
2x4=8 _____	zwei mal vier ist acht *tsvai marl fear ist akht*
4÷2=2 _____	vier geteilt durch zwei ist zwei *fear getailt doorkh tsvai ist tsvai*
odd/even _____	gerade/ungerarde *gerarder/oongerader*
total _____	(ins)gesamt *(ins)gezammt*
6x9 _____	sechs mal neun *zekhs marl noyn*

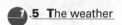

Is the weather going to be good/bad?	Wird das Wetter schön/schlecht? _virt dass vetter shoen/shlekht?_	
Is it going to get colder/hotter?	Wird es kälter/wärmer? _virt es kaelter/vaermer?_	
What temperature is it going to be?	Wieviel Grad wird es? _veefeel grart virt ez?_	
Is it going to rain?	Wird es regnen? _virt ez raygnen?_	
Is there going to be a storm?	Bekommen wir Sturm? _bekommen veer shturm?_	
Is it going to snow?	Wird es schneien? _virt es shnaien?_	
Is it going to freeze?	Wird es frieren? _virt es freeren?_	
Is the thaw setting in?	Wird es tauen? _virt es towen?_	
Is it going to be foggy?	Bekommen wir Nebel? _bekommen veer naybel?_	
Is there going to be a thunderstorm?	Wird es ein Gewitter geben? _virt es ain gevitter gayben?_	
The weather's changing	Das Wetter schlägt um _dass vetter shlaekt oom_	
It's cooling down	Es kühlt sich ab _ez kuehlt zikh ap_	
What's the weather going to be like today	Was für Wetter wird heute? _vass fuer vetter virt hoyter?_	

Bewölkung cloud	kalt cold	Rückenwind tail wind
Böen squalls	klar clear	Schnee snow
frisch chilly (temperature), fresh (wind)	kühl chilly	schwül muggy
	leicht bewölkt cloudy	sehr heiss scorching hot
Frost frost	leichte Bewölkung light clouds	sonnig sunny
Glatteis black ice	mild mild	Sprühregen drizzle
... Grad (unter/über Null) ... degrees (above/below zero)	nasskalt cold and damp	stark bewölkt overcast
	Nebel fog	starke Bewölkung heavy clouds
Graupel/Hagel hail	Orkan hurricane	Sturm storm
heiter fine	rauh bleak	Wind (leichter/ mässiger/starker) light/moderate/strong wind
heiss hot	Regenschauer shower	windig windy
Hitzewelle heat wave	Regen(schauer) rain	

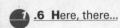

Useful lists

.6 Here, there...

See also 5.1 Asking for directions

here/there	hier/da
	heer/dar
somewhere/nowhere	irgendwo/nirgendwo
	eergentvoa/neergentvoa
everywhere	überall
	ueberall
far away/nearby	weit weg/inder Nähe
	vait vek/in dayr nayher
right/left	nach rechts/links
	nakh rekhts/links
to the right/left of	rechts/links von
	rekhts/links fon
straight ahead	geradeaus
	gerarder ows
via	über
	ueber
in	in
	in
on	auf
	owf
under	unter
	oonter
against	gegen
	gaygen
opposite	gegenüber
	gaygen ueber
next to	neben
	nayben
near	bei
	bai
in front of	vor
	for
in the centre	in der Mitte
	in dayr mitter
forward	nach vorn
	nakh forn
down	(nach) unten
	(nakh) oonten
up	(nach) oben
	(nakh) owben
inside	drinnen
	drinnen
outside	draussen/raus
	drowssen/rows
behind	(nach) hinten
	(nakh) hinten
at the front	vorn
	forn
at the back	hinten
	hinten
in the north	im Norden
	im norden

to the south	nach Süden	*nakh zueden*
from the west	aus dem Westen	*ows dem vesten*
from the east	aus dem Osten	*ows daym ossten*
north, east, south, west of	nördlich/östlich/südlich/westlich von	*noerdlikh/oestlikh/zuedlikh/vestlikh fon*

.7 What does that sign say?

See 5.4 Traffic signs

Abfahrt	exit
Achtung	beware
Ankunft	arrival
Aufzug	lift
Ausgang	exit
Auskunft	information
Bahnhof	station
Bitte nicht stören	Do not disturb
Drücken	push
Durchgang	throughway
Eingang	entrance
Eintritt frei/verboten	free entry/no entry
Empfang	reception
Erste Hilfe	first aid
Fahrkarten	tickets
Fahrstuhl	lift
Freibad	open-air swimming-pool
Fremdenverkehrsverein	tourist information
Fussgänger	pedestrians
Gasthaus/Gasthof	inn
Gefahr	danger
Geöffnet	open
Gepäckannahme/-aufbewahrung	check-in/left-luggage
Geschlossen	closed
Gleis	platform
Hausmeister	caretaker
Herein!	Come in!
Kein Trinkwasser	No drinking water
Nicht berühren!	Please do not touch!
Notausgang/-treppe	emergency exit/stairs
Öffnungszeiten	opening hours
Pförtner	porter
Polizei	police
Rathaus	town hall/city hall
Rauchen verboten	no smoking
Reserviert	reserved
Rundfahrt	tour
Schliessfach	left luggage locker/safe deposit box
Schwimmbad	swimming-pool
Selbstbedienung	self-service
Stock	floor
Treppe	stairs
Vorsicht!	beware
Warnung	beware/warning
Warteraum/-saal	waiting room
Wechselstube	exchange office
Ziehen	pull
Zimmer frei/zu vermieten	vacancy (room)/room to let
Zugang	access/entry

Useful lists

.8 Telephone alphabet

a	ar	wie Anton	*vee arnton*
ä	ay	wie Ärger	*vee airger*
b	beh	wie Berta	*vee berter*
c	tseh	wie Cäsar	*vee tsezer*
ch	tseh-har	wie Charlotte	*vee sharlotter*
d	deh	wie Dora	*vee doara*
e	eh	wie Emil	*vee aymil*
f	ef	wie Friedrich	*vee freedrikh*
g	geh	wie Gustav	*vee goostaf*
h	hah	wie Heinrich	*vee hainrikh*
i	ee	wie Ida	*vee eeda*
j	yot	wie Julius	*vee yoolius*
k	kah	wie Kaufmann	*vee kowfmann*
l	el	wie Ludwig	*vee loodvikh*
m	em	wie Martha	*vee marta*
n	en	wie Nordpol	*vee nortpole*
o	oh	wie Otto	*vee ottoa*
ö	oe	wie Ökonom	*vee oekonoam*
p	peh	wie Paula	*vee powla*
q	koo	wie Quelle	*vee kveller*
r	air	wie Richard	*vee rikhart*
sch	es-tseh-har	wie Schule	*vee shooler*
s	es	wie Samuel	*vee zarmooel*
t	teh	wie Theodor	*vee tayoador*
u	oo	wie Ulrich	*vee oolrikh*
ü	ue	wie Übermut	*vee uebermoot*
v	fow	wie Viktor	*vee viktor*
w	veh	wie Wilhelm	*vee vilhelm*
x	iks	wie Xanthippe	*vee ksantippeh*
y	uepsilon	wie Ypsilon	*vee uepsilon*
z	tset	wie Zacharias	*vee tsakharias*

.9 Personal details

surname	(der) Nachname
	(dayr) nakhnarmer
christian name	(der) Vorname
	(dayr) fornarmer
initials	(der) Anfangsbuchstabe des Vornamens
	(dayr) an-fangs-bookh-shtarber dess fornarmenz
address (street/ number)	(die) Anschrift (Strasse/Nummer)
	(dee) anshrift (shtrasser/noommer)
post code/town	(die) Postleitzahl/(der) Wohnort
	(dee) posst-lait-tsarl/(dayr) voanort
sex (male/female)	(das) Geschlecht (m.= männlich, w.= weiblich)
	(dass) geschlekht (m.= maennlikh, w. = vaiblikh)
nationality	(die) Staatsangehörigkeit
	(dee) shtarts-ange-hoerikh-kait
date of birth	(das) Geburtsdatum
	(dass) geboorts dartum

place of birth _____	(der) Geburtsort
	(dayr) geboorts ort
occupation _____	(der) Beruf
	(dayr) beroof
married/single/ _____ divorced	verheiratet/ledig/geschieden
	fairhai-rartet/laydikh/gescheeden
widowed _____	(die) Witwe/(der) Witwer
	(dee) vitveh/ (dayr) vitver
(number of) children _____	(Zahl der) Kinder
	(tsarl dayr) kinder
identity card/passport/ _____ driving licence number	Personalausweis/Reisepass/Führerschein-nummer,
	pair zoanarl owsvaiz-raizerparss/fuerershain-nummer
place and date of issue ____	Ort und Datum der Ausstellung
	ort oont dartoom dayr owsshtelloong

Courtesies

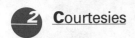 **Courtesies**

● **It is usual in Germany** to shake hands on meeting and parting company.

 .1 Greetings

● **The correct pronoun** to use in formal greetings is '*Sie*' (zee) - which translates as 'you' - in the singular and plural. '*Sie*' should be employed when addressing people over the age of 18 except when talking to intimates. Conversation within the family, or between children, youths, students, friends and close work colleagues requires the use of the familiar second person pronoun '*du*' (doo). Please note that amongst adults it is usual for the older person to offer the more familiar address of '*du*' to the younger one.

Hello, Mr...	Guten Tag, Herr...
	gooten tark, hair...
Hello, Mrs...	Guten Tag, Frau...
	gooten tark, frow...
Hello, Peter	Hallo, Peter
	hallo, payter
Hi, Helen	Tag, Helene
	tark, helayner
Good morning	Guten Morgen
	gooten morgen
Good afternoon	Guten Tag
	gooten tark
Good evening	Guten Abend
	gooten arbent
How are you?	Wie geht's?
	vee gayts?
Fine, thank you, and you?	Sehr gut, und Ihnen?
	zayr goot, oont eenen?
Very well	Ausgezeichnet
	ows ge tsaikh net
Not very well	Nicht besonders
	nikht bezonderz
Not too bad	Es geht
	ez gayt
I'd better be going	Dann geh' ich mal
	dann gay' ikh mall
I have to be going.	Ich muss los. Ich werde erwartet
Someone's waiting for me	*ikh mooss loas. ikh verder ervartet*
Bye!	Tschüs
	tshuess
Goodbye	Auf Wiedersehen
	owf veederzayn
See you soon	Bis bald
	biss balt
See you later	Bis gleich
	biss glaich
See you in a little while	Bis dann
	biss dann
Sleep well	Schlafen Sie gut
	shlarfen zee goot

Good night _____	Gute Nacht
	gooter nakht
All the best _____	Alles Gute
	alles gooter
Have fun _____	Viel Vergnügen
	feel fairgnuegen
Good luck _____	Viel Glück
	feel gluek
Have a nice holiday _____	(Einen) schönen Urlaub
	(ainen) shoenen oorlowp
Have a good trip _____	Gute Reise
	gooter raizer
Thank you, you too _____	Danke, gleichfalls
	danker, glaikhfalz
Say hello to...for me _____	Schöne Grüsse an...
	shoener gruesser an...

2.2 How to ask a question

Who? _____	Wer?
	vayr?
Who's that? _____	Wer ist das?
	vayr ist dass?
What? _____	Was?
	vass?
What's there to _____ see here?	Was gibt es hier zu sehen?
	vass gipt ez heer tsoo zayhen?
What kind of hotel _____ is that?	Was für eine Art Hotel ist das?
	vass fuer ainer art hotel ist dass?
Where? _____	Wo?
	voe?
Where's the toilet? _____	Wo ist die Toilette?
	voe ist dee twaletter?
Where are you going? _____	Wohin gehen/(by car) fahren Sie?
	vohin gayhen/fahren zee?
Where are you from? _____	Woher kommen Sie?
	vohair kommen zee?
How? _____	Wie?
	vee?
How far is that? _____	Wie weit ist das?
	vee vait ist dass?
How long does that take? ___	Wie lange dauert das?
	vee langer dowert dass?
How long is the trip? _____	Wie lange dauert die Reise?
	vee langer dowert dee raizer?
How much? _____	Wieviel?
	veefeel?
How much is this? _____	Wieviel kostet das?
	veefeel kostet dass?
What time is it? _____	Wie spät ist es?
	vee shpayt ist ez?
Which? _____	Welcher (masculine), welches (neuter), welche (feminine, plural)
	velkher? velkherz? velkher?
Which glass is mine? _____	Welches Glas ist für mich?
	velkherz glars ist fuer mikh?

When? _____ Wann?
vann?

When are you leaving? ____ Wann reisen Sie ab?
vann raizen zee ap?

Why?_____ Warum?
vahroom?

Could you...me?_____ Können Sie mir/mich...
koennen zee meer/mikh...

Could you help me, _____ Könnten Sie mir bitte helfen?
please? *koennten zee meer bitter helfen?*

Could you point that_____ Können Sie mir das zeigen?
out to me? *koennen zee meer dass tsaygen?*

Could you come _____ Würden Sie bitte mit mir mitgehen?
with me, please? *vuerden zee bitter mit meer mitgayhen?*

Could you..._____ Würden Sie bitte...?
vuerden zee bitter...?

Could you reserve some ___ Würden Sie bitte Karten für mich
tickets for me, please? reservieren?
*vuerden zee bitter karten fuer mikh
rozorveeren?*

Do you know...? Wissen Sie...?
vissen zee...?

Do you know another_____ Könnten Sie mir ein anderes Hotel
hotel, please? empfehlen?
*koennten zee meer ain anderez hotel
empfaylen?*

Do you know whether...?___ Wissen Sie ob..
vissen zee op...

Do you have a...?_____ Haben Sie ein(en)/eine...?
harben zee ain(en)/ainor...?

Do you have a _____ Haben Sie bitte ein vegetarisches Gericht?
vegetarian dish, please? *harben zee bitter ain vegetarishers
gerikht?*

I'd like... _____ Ich möchte gern ...
ikh moekhter gayrn ...

I'd like a kilo of apples, ___ Ich möchte bitte ein Kilo Äpfel
please. *ikh moekhter bitter ain kilo epfel*

Can I...?_____ Darf ich...?
darf ikh...?

Can I take this?_____ Darf ich dies mitnehmen?
darf ikh dees mittnaymen?

Can I smoke here?_____ Darf ich hier rauchen?
darf ikh heer rowkhen?

Could I ask you _____ Darf ich Sie etwas fragen?
something? *darf ikh zee etvass frargen?*

2 Courtesies

2 .3 How to reply

Yes, of course _____	Ja, natürlich *yar, natuerlikh*
No, I'm sorry _____	Nein, es tut mir leid *Nain, ez toot meer lait*
Yes, what can I do for you?	Ja, was kann ich für Sie tun? *yar, vass kann ikh fuer zee toon?*
Just a moment, please ____	Einen Augenblick bitte *ainen owgen blick bitter*
No, I don't have time now	Nein, ich habe jetzt keine Zeit *nain, ikh haber yetst kainer tsait*
No, that's impossible _____	Nein, das ist unmöglich *nain, dass ist oonmoeglikh*
I think so _____	Ich glaube schon *ikh glowber shoan*
I agree _____	Ich glaube (es) auch *ikh glowber (ez) owkh*
I hope so too _____	Ich hoffe (es) auch *ikh hoffer (ez) owkh*
No, not at all _____	Nein, überhaupt nicht *nain, ueberhowpt nikht*
No, no-one _____	Nein, niemand *nain, neemant*
No, nothing _____	Nein, nichts *nain, nikhts*
That's (not) right _____	Das stimmt (nicht) *dass shtimmt (nikht)*
I (don't) agree _____	Da stimme ich Ihnen (nicht) zu *dar shtimmer ikh eenen (nikht) tsoo*
Okay _____	Einverstanden *ain-fair-shtanden*
Perhaps _____	vielleicht *feelaikht*
I don't know _____	Ich weiss es nicht *ikh vaiss es nikht*

2 .4 Thank you

Thank you _____	Vielen Dank *feelen dunk*
You're welcome _____	Keine Ursache/gern geschehen *kainer oorzakher/gayrn geshayhen*
Thank you very much ____	Vielen herzlichen Dank *feelen hairtslikhen dunk*
Very kind of you _____	Sehr freundlich (von Ihnen) *zayr froyntlikh (fon eenen)*
I enjoyed it very much ____	Es war mir ein Vergnügen *es var meer ain fairgnuegen*
Thank you for your trouble	Ich danke Ihnen für die Mühe *ikh dunker eenen fuer dee muer*
You shouldn't have _____	Das wäre nicht nötig gewesen *dass vayrer nikht noetikh gevayzen*
That's all right _____	Ist schon in Ordnung *ist shoan in ordnoong*

2.5 Sorry

Excuse me	Verzeihung *fair tsaioong*
Sorry!	Entschuldigung *ent shool digoong*
I'm sorry, I didn't know...	Entschuldigung, ich wusste nicht, dass... *ent shool digung, ikh vuster nihkt dass...*
I do apologise	Ich bitte vielmals um Verzeihung *ikh bitter feelmarls oom fair tsaioong*
Please don't hold it against me	Nehmen Sie (es) mir bitte nicht übel *naymen zee (es) meer bitter nihkt uebel*
I'm sorry	Es tut mir leid *ez toot meer lait*
I didn't do it on purpose, it was an accident	Ich habe es nicht mit Absicht getan, es war ein Versehen *ikh harber ez nihkt mit apsikht getarn, ez var ain fairzayhen*
That's all right	Das macht nichts *dass makht nihkts*
Never mind	Lassen Sie nur *lassen zee noor*
It could've happened to anyone	Das kann jedem mal passieren *dass kann yaydem marl passeeren*

2.6 What do you think?

Which do you prefer?	Was ist Ihnen lieber? *vass ist eenen leeber?*
What do you think?	Was halten Sie davon? *vass harlten zee dafonn?*
I don't mind	Es ist mir egal *ez ist meer egarl*
Well done!	Sehr gut! *zayr goot!*
Not bad!	Nicht schlecht! *nikht shlekht!*
Great!	Ausgezeichnet! *ows ge tsaykh net!*
It's really nice here!	Hier ist es aber gemütlich! *heer ist ez arber gemuetlikh!*
How nice for you!	Wie hübsch/schön (für Sie/dich)! *vee huepsh/shoen (fuer zee/dikh)!*
I'm (not) very happy with...	Ich bin (nicht) sehr zufrieden über... *ikh bin (nikht) zayr tsoofreeden ueber...*
I'm glad...	Ich bin froh, dass... *ikh bin froa, dass...*
I'm having a great time	Ich amüsiere mich sehr gut *ikh amuezeerer mikh zayr goot*
I'm looking forward to it	Ich freue mich drauf *ikh froyer mikh drowf*
Impossible	Unmöglich! *oonmoeglikh!*
That's terrible!	Wie scheußlich! *vee shoysslikh!*

2

Courtesies

What a pity! _____ Wie schade!
vee sharder!

That's filthy! _____ Wie schmutzig/dreckig!
vee shmootsikh/drekkikh!

What a load of rubbish! ___ (So'n) Quatsch!
(zoan) kvatsh!

I don't like... _____ Ich mag kein/keine(n) (+ noun)/Ich (+ verb)
nicht gern
ikh mark kain/kainer(n)/ikh...nikht gayrn

I'm bored to death _____ Ich langweile mich furchtbar
ikh langvailer mikh foorkhtbar

I've had enough _____ Mir reicht's
meer raikhts

I was expecting _____ Ich hatte etwas ganz anderes erwartet
something completely *ikh hatter etvass gants andererz airvartet*
different

Conversation

Conversation

3 .1 I beg your pardon?

I don't speak any/	Ich spreche kein/ein bisschen...
I speak a little...	*ikh shprekher kain/ain bisskhen...*
I'm English	Ich bin Engländer/in
	ikh bin englender (male)/englenderin (female)
I'm Scottish	Ich bin Schotte/Schottin
	ikh bin shotter/shottin
I'm Irish	Ich bin Irländer/Irländerin
	ikh bin earlender/earlenderin
I'm Welsh	Ich bin Waliser/Waliserin
	ikh bin valeezer/valeezerin
Do you speak	Sprechen Sie
English/French/German?	Englisch/Französisch/Deutsch?
	shprekhen zee english/frantsoezish/doytsh?
Is there anyone who	Ist hier jemand, der ... spricht?
speaks...?	*ist heer yaymant, dayr ... shprikht?*
I beg your pardon?	Wie bitte?
	vee bitter?
I (don't) understand	Ich verstehe (es) (nicht)
	ikh fair shtayher (es) (nikht)
Do you understand me?	Verstehen Sie mich?
	fair shtayhen zee mikh?
Could you repeat that,	Würden Sie das bitte wiederholen?
please?	*vuerden zee dass bitter vee-der-hoalen?*
Could you speak more	Könnten Sie etwas langsamer sprechen?
slowly, please?	*koennten zee etvass langzarmer shprekhen?*
What does that (word)	Was bedeutet das/dieses Wort?
mean?	*vass bedoytet dass/deezez vort?*
Is that similar to/the	Ist das (ungefähr) dasselbe wie..?
same as...?	*ist dass (oongefair) dass zelber vee..?*
Could you write that	Könnten Sie mir das bitte aufschreiben?
down for me, please?	*koennten zee meer dass bitter owfshraiben?*
Could you spell that	Könnten Sie mir das bitte buchstabieren?
for me, please?	*koennten zee meer dass bitter bookhshtabeeren?*

(See 1.8 Telephone alphabet)

Could you point that	Könnten Sie mir das in diesem
out in this phrase book,	Sprachführer zeigen?
please?	*koennten zee meer dass in deezem shprakhfuerer tsaigen?*
One moment, please,	Augenblick bitte, ich muß es erst suchen
I have to look it up	*owgenblick bitte, ikh mooss ez erst zookhen*
I can't find the word/the	Ich kann das Wort/den Satz nicht finden
sentence	*ikh kann dass vort/dayn zats nikht finden*
How do you say	Wie sagt man das auf...
that in...?	*vee zarkt mann dass owf...*
How do you pronounce	Wie spricht man das aus?
that?	*vee shprikht mann dass ows?*

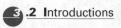

3.2 Introductions

May I introduce myself?	Darf ich mich Ihnen vorstellen? *darf ikh mikh eenen forshtellen?*
My name's...	Ich heisse... *ikh haisser...*
I'm...	Ich bin... *ikh bin...*
What's your name?	Wie heissen Sie? *vee haissen zee?*
May I introduce...?	Darf ich Ihnen vorstellen...? *darf ikh eenen forshtellen...?*
This is my wife/daughter/mother/girlfriend	Dies ist meine Frau/Tochter/Mutter/Freundin *deez ist mainer frow/tokhter/mootter/froyndin*
– my husband/son/father/boyfriend	Dies ist mein Mann/Sohn/Vater/Freund. *dees ist main mann/zoan/farter/froynt.*
How do you do	Guten Tag/Abend, nett Sie kennenzulernen *gooten tark/arbent, nett zee kennen tsoo layrnen*
Pleased to meet you	Angenehm *angenaym*
Where are you from?	Woher kommen Sie? *voahair kommen zee?*
I'm from England/Scotland/Ireland/Wales	Ich komme aus England/Schottland/Irland/Wales *ikh kommer ows englant/shottlant/eerlant/vaylz*
What city do you live in?	In welcher Stadt wohnen Sie? *in velkher shtatt voanen zee?*
In..., It is near...	In.... Das ist in der Nähe von... *in... dass ist in dayr nayher fon...*
Have you been here long?	Sind Sie schon lange hier? *zint zee shoan langer heer?*
A few days	Ein paar Tage *ain pahr targer*
How long are you staying here?	Wie lange bleiben Sie hier? *vee langer blaiben zee heer?*
We're (probably) leaving tomorrow/in two weeks	Wir reisen (wahrscheinlich) morgen/in zwei Wochen ab *veer raizen (varshainlikh) morgun/in tsvai vokhen ap*
Where are you staying?	Wo wohnen Sie? *vo voanen zee?*
In a hotel/an apartment	In einem Hotel/Appartement *in ainem hotel/apartament*
On a camp site	Auf einem Campingplatz *owf ainem camping plats*
With friends/relatives	Bei Freunden/Verwandten *bai froynden/fairvanten*
Are you here on your own/with your family?	Sind Sie hier allein/mit Ihrer Familie? *zint zee heer allain/mit eerer fameelyeh?*
I'm on my own	Ich bin allein *ikh bin allain*

I'm with my_____ partner/wife/husband	Ich bin hier mit meinem Partner/meiner Partnerin/meiner Frau/meinem Mann *ikh bin heer mit mainem partner/mainer partnerin/mainer frow/mainem man*
– with my family _____	Ich bin hier mit meiner Familie *ikh bin hier mit mainer fameelyeh*
– with relatives _____	Ich bin hier mit Verwandten *ikh bin hier mit fairvanten*
– with a friend/friends _____	Ich bin hier mit einem Freund/einer Freundin/Freunden *ikh bin hier mit ainem froynt/ainer froyndin/froynden*
Are you married? _____	Sind Sie verheiratet? *zint zee fairhairartet?*
Do you have a steady _____ boyfriend/girlfriend?	Hast du eine feste Freundin/einen festen Freund? *hast doo ainer fester froyndin/aynen festen froynt?*
That's none of your _____ business	Das geht Sie nichts an *dass gayt zee nikhts an*
I'm married_____	Ich bin verheiratet *ikh bin fairhai rartet*
– single_____	Ich bin Junggeselle/Junggesellin *ikh bin yoong ge zeller/yoong ge zellin*
– separated _____	Ich lebe getrennt *ikh layber getrennt*
– divorced _____	Ich bin geschieden *ikh bin gesheeden*
– a widow/widower _____	Ich bin Witwe/Witwer *ikh bin vitveh/vitver*
I live alone/with _____ someone	Ich lebe allein/mit jemandem zusammen *ikh layber allain/mit yaymandem tsoozammen*
Do you have any_____ children/grandchildren?	Haben Sie Kinder/Enkel? *harben zee kinder/enkell?*
How old are you? _____	Wie alt sind Sie? *vee alt zint zee?*
How old is he/she? _____	Wie alt ist er/sie? *vee alt ist ayr/zee?*
I'm... _____	Ich bin ... Jahre alt *ikh bin ... yahrer alt*
She's/he's... _____	Sie/er ist ... Jahre alt *zee/ayr ist ... yahrer alt*
What do you do for a_____ living?	Was für eine Arbeit machen Sie? *vass fuer ainer arbait makhen zee?*
I work in an office _____	Ich arbeite in einem Büro *ikh arbaiter in ainem buero*
I'm a student/_____ I'm at school	Ich studiere/gehe zur Schule *ikh shtoodearer/gayher tsoor shooler*
I'm unemployed _____	Ich bin arbeitslos *ikh bin arbaitsloaz*
I'm retired_____	Ich bin pensioniert/Rentner/Rentnerin *ikh bin pen zeeoa neert/rentner/rentnerin*
I have taken early _____ retirement	Ich bin im Vorruhestand *ikh bin im for-roohor shtant*
I'm on a disability _____ pension	Ich habe eine Erwerbsunfähigkeitsrente *ikh harber ainer erverps oon fayikh kaits renter*

28

I'm a housewife	Ich bin Hausfrau
	ikh bin howzfrow
Do you like your job?	Macht Ihnen die Arbeit Spass?
	makht eenen dee arbait shpass?
Most of the time	Mal ja, mal nein
	marl yar, marl nain
I usually do, but I prefer holidays	Meistens schon, aber Urlaub ist schöner
	maistens shoan, arber oorlowp ist shoener

3 .3 Starting/ending a conversation

Could I ask you something?	Dürfte ich Sie etwas fragen?
	duerfter ikh zee etvass fragren?
Excuse me	Entschuldigen Sie bitte
	ent shool digen zee bitter
Excuse me, could you help me?	Entschuldigung, könnten Sie mir helfen?
	ent shool digoong, koennten zee meer helfen?
Yes, what's the problem?	Ja, was ist denn los?
	yar, vass ist den loas?
What can I do for you?	Was kann ich für Sie tun?
	vass kan ikh fuer zee toon?
Sorry, I don't have time now	Bedaure, ich habe jetzt keine Zeit
	bedowrer, ikh harber yetst kainer tsayt
Do you have a light?	Haben Sie Feuer?
	harben zee foyerr?
May I join you?	Darf ich mich zu Ihnen setzen?
	darf ikh mikh tsoo eenen zetsen?
Could you take a picture of me/us?	Würden Sie ein Foto von mir/uns machen?
	vuerden zee ain foto fon meer/oons makhen?
Leave me alone	Lassen Sie mich in Ruhe
	lassen zee mikh in rooher
Get lost	Machen Sie, daß Sie wegkommen
	makhen zee dass zee vek kommen
Go away or I'll scream	Wenn Sie nicht weggehen, schrei' ich
	ven zee nikht vek gayhen, shrai ikh

3 .4 Congratulations and condolences

Happy birthday/many happy returns	Meinen Glückwunsch zum Geburtstag
	mainen gluekvoonsh tsoom geboortstark
Please accept my condolences	Mein Beileid
	main bailait
I'm very sorry for you	Es tut mir ja so leid für Sie
	ez toot meer yar zo lait fuer zee

3 .5 A chat about the weather

See also 1.5 The weather

It's so hot/cold today!	Heute ist es aber warm/kalt!
	hoyter ist ez arber varm/kalt!
Nice weather, isn't it?	Angenehmes Wetter, nicht?
	angenaymers vetter, nikht?
What a wind/storm!	So ein Wind/Sturm!
	zo ain vint/shtoorm

All that rain/snow!	Wie das regnet/schneit! *vee dass raygnet/shnait!*
All that fog!	Das ist vielleicht ein Nebel! *dass ist feelaikht ain naybel!*
Has the weather been like this for long here?	Ist das Wetter hier schon lange so? *ist dass vetter heer shoan langer zo?*
Is it always this hot/cold here?	Ist es hier immer so warm/kalt? *ist es heer immer zo varm/kalt?*
Is it always this dry/wet here?	Ist es hier immer so trocken/nass? *ist es heer immer zo trokken/nass?*

3.6 Hobbies

Do you have any hobbies?	Haben Sie Hobbys? *harben zee hobbies?*
I like knitting/reading/photography/painting	Ich stricke/lese/fotografiere/zeichne gern *ikh shtrikker/layzer/fotograffearer/tsaikhner gayrn*
I like music	Ich liebe Musik *ikh leeber moozeek*
I like playing the guitar/piano	Ich spiele gern Gitarre/Klavier *ikh shpeeler gayrn gitarrer/klaveer*
I like going to the movies	Ich gehe gern ins Kino *ikh gayher gayrn ins keeno*
I like travelling/fishing/walking/sport	Ich reise/angle/wandre gern *ikh raizer/angler/vanderer gayrn*

3.7 Being the host(ess)

See also 4 Eating out

Can I offer you a drink?	Darf ich Ihnen etwas zu trinken anbieten? *darf ikh eenen etvass tsoo trinken anbeeten?*
What would you like to drink?	Was möchtest du trinken? *vass moekhtest doo trinken?*
Would you like a cigarette/cigar?	Möchten Sie eine Zigarette/Zigarre? *moekhten zee ainer tsigarretter/tsigarrer?*
Something non-alcoholic, please	Gern etwas ohne Alkohol *gayrn etvass oaner alkohol*
I don't smoke	Ich rauche nicht *ikh rowkher nikht*

3.8 Invitations

Are you doing anything tonight?	Hast du heute abend was vor? *hast doo hoyter arbent vass for?*
Do you have any plans for today/this afternoon/tonight?	Haben Sie schon Pläne für heute/heute nachmittag/heute abend? *harben zee shoan playner fuer hoyter/hoyter nakhmittark/hoyter arbent?*
Would you like to go out with me?	Haben Sie Lust, mit mir auszugehen? *harben zee loost, mit meer ows tsoo gayhen?*
Would you like to go dancing with me?	Haben Sie Lust, mit mir tanzen zu gehen? *harben zee loost, mitt meer tantsen tsoo gayhen?*

Conversation

Would you like to have ____ lunch/dinner with me?	Haben Sie Lust, mit mir zu essen?
	harben zee loost, mit meer tsoo essen?
Would you like to come____ to the beach with me?	Haben Sie Lust, an den Strand zu gehen?
	harben zee loost, an den shtrant tsoo gayhen?
Would you like to come____ into town with us?	Haben Sie Lust, mit uns in die Stadt zu gehen/fahren?
	harben zee loost, mit oons in dee shtatt tsoo gayhen/fahren?
Would you like to come____ and see some friends with us?	Haben Sie Lust, mit uns zu Freunden zu gehen?
	harben zee loost, mit oons tsoo froynden tsoo gayhen?
Shall we dance?_____	Wollen wir tanzen?
	vollen veer tantsen?
– sit at the bar? _____	Kommst du mit an die Bar?
	kommst doo mit an dee bar?
– get something to drink?__	Wollen wir etwas trinken?
	vollen veer etvass trinken?
– go for a walk/drive?_____	Wollen wir ein bisschen spazierengehen/Auto fahren?
	vollen veer ain bisskhen shpatseeren gayhen/owto fahren?
Yes, all right _____	Ja, gut
	yar, goot
Good idea _____	Gute Idee
	gooter eeday
No (thank you) _____	Nein (danke)
	nain (dunker)
Maybe later_____	Vielleicht später
	feelaikht shpayter
I don't feel like it _____	Dazu habe ich keine Lust
	datsoo harber ikh kainer loost
I don't have time _____	Ich habe keine Zeit
	ikh harber kainer tsait
I already have a date _____	Ich habe schon eine Verabredung
	ikh harber shoan ainer fair ap ray doong
I'm not very good at_____ dancing/volleyball/ swimming	Ich kann nicht tanzen/Volleyball spielen/schwimmen
	ikh kann nikht tantsen/volleyball shpeelen/shvimmen

3.9 Paying a compliment

You look wonderful! _____	Sie sehen (ja) fabelhaft aus!
	zee zayhen (yar) farbelhaft ows!
I like your car! _____	Schönes/tolles Auto!
	shoenez/tollez owto!
I like your ski outfit! _____	Hübscher Skianzug!
	huepsher shee antsook!
You're a nice boy/girl _____	Du bist lieb
	doo bist leep
What a sweet child! _____	Was für ein liebes Kind!
	vass fuer ain leebes kint!
You're a wonderful _____ dancer!	Sie tanzen sehr gut!
	zee tantsen zayr goot!

31

You're a wonderful cook!	Sie kochen sehr gut!
	zee kokhen zayr goot!
You're a terrific soccer player!	Sie spielen sehr gut Fussball!
	zee shpeelen zayr goot foossball!

3.10 Chatting someone up

I like being with you	Ich bin gern mit dir zusammen
	ikh bin gayrn mit deer tsoozammen
I've missed you so much	Ich habe dich so vermisst
	ikh haber dikh zo fairmisst
I dreamt about you	Ich habe von dir geträumt
	ikh haber fon deer getroymt
I think about you all day	Ich muss den ganzen Tag an dich denken
	ikh muss den gantsen tark an dikh denken
You have such a sweet smile	Du lächelst so süss
	doo laekhelst zo suess
You have such beautiful eyes	Du hast so schöne Augen
	doo hast zo shoener owgen
I'm in love with you	Ich habe mich in dich verliebt
	ikh haber mikh in dikh fairleept
I'm in love with you too	Ich mich auch in dich
	ikh mikh owkh in dikh
I love you	Ich liebe dich
	ikh leeber dikh
I love you too	Ich dich auch
	ikh dikh owkh
I don't feel as strongly about you	Ich empfinde nicht dasselbe für dich
	ikh empfinder nikht dass selber fuer dikh
I already have a boyfriend/girlfriend	Ich habe schon einen Freund/eine Freundin
	ikh harber shoan ainen froynt/ainer froyndin
I'm not ready for that	Ich bin noch nicht so weit
	ikh bin nokh nikht zo vait
This is going too fast for me	Es geht mir viel zu schnell
	ez gayt meer feel tsoo shnell
Take your hands off me	Rühr mich nicht an
	ruehr mikh nikht an
Okay, no problem	O.k., kein Problem
	oakay, kain problaym
Will you stay with me tonight?	Bleibst du heute nacht bei mir?
	blaipst doo hoyter nakht bai meer?
I'd like to go to bed with you	Ich möchte mit dir schlafen
	ikh moekhter mit deer shlarfen
Only if we use a condom	Nur mit Präservativ/Kondom
	noor mitt prezervatif/kondoam
We have to be careful about AIDS	Wir müssen vorsichtig sein wegen Aids
	veer muessen forsikhtikh zain vaygen aids
That's what they all say	Das sagen alle
	dass zargen aller
We shouldn't take any risks	Wir wollen lieber kein Risiko eingehen
	veer vollen leeber kain reeziko aingayhen
Do you have a condom?	Hast du ein Präservativ/Kondom?
	hast doo ain prezervatif/kondoam?
No? In that case we won't do it	Nein? Dann machen wir's nicht
	nain? dann makhen veer's nikht

3.11 Arrangements

When will I see you again?	Wann sehe ich Sie/dich wieder? *vann zayher ikh zee/dikh veeder?*
Are you free over the weekend?	Haben Sie am Wochenende Zeit? *harben zee am vokhenender tsait?*
What shall we arrange?	Wie verbleiben wir? *vee fairblaiben veer?*
Where shall we meet?	Wo wollen wir uns treffen? *voa vollen veer oons treffen?*
Will you pick me/us up?	Holen Sie mich/uns ab? *hoalen zee mikh/oons ap?*
Shall I pick you up?	Soll ich Sie abholen? *zoll ikh zee apholen?*
I have to be home by...	Ich muss um...Uhr zu Hause sein *ikh muss oom...ooer tsoo howzer zain*
I don't want to see you anymore	Ich will Sie nicht mehr sehen *ikh vill zee nikht mayr zayhen*

3.12 Saying goodbye

Can I take you home?	Darf ich Sie nach Hause bringen? *darf ikh zee nakh howzer bringen?*
Can I write/call you?	Darf ich Ihnen schreiben/Sie anrufen? *darf ikh eenen shraiben/zee anroofen?*
Will you write/call me?	Schreiben Sie mir/rufen Sie mich an? *shraiben zee meer/roofen zee mikh an?*
Can I have your address/phone number?	Geben Sie mir Ihre Adresse/Telefonnummer? *gayben zee meer eerer adresser/telefoan noomer?*
Thanks for everything	Vielen Dank für alles *feelen dunk fuer alless*
It was very nice	Es war sehr schön *es var zayr shoen*
Say hello to...	Grüssen Sie... *gruessen zee...*
All the best	Alles Gute *alles gooter*
Good luck	Viel Erfolg weiter *feel erfolk vaiter*
When will you be back?	Wann kommst du wieder? *vann kommst doo veeder?*
I'll be waiting for you	Ich warte auf dich *ikh varter owf dikh*
I'd like to see you again	Ich möchte dich gern wiedersehen *ikh moekhter dikh gayrn veeder zayhen*
I hope we meet again soon	Ich hoffe, wir sehen uns wieder *ikh hoffer, veer zayhen oons veeder*
This is our address. If you're ever in the UK...	Dies ist unsere Adresse. Wenn Sie je in Grossbritannien sind... *deez ist oonzerer adresser. venn zee yay in englant zint...*
You'd be more than welcome	Sie sind uns herzlich willkommen *zee zint oons hertslikh villkommen*

Eating out

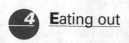

4 Eating out

● **In Germany** people usually have three main meals:

1 *Frühstück* (breakfast) between approx. 6.30 and 10 am. Breakfast is varied and can consist of coffee or herbal infusions, cereal (particularly muesli), bread rolls or slices of *Vollkornbrot* (whole-wheat bread) with a choice of butter, jam, ham or cheese. On Sundays this array is often complemented by boiled eggs.

2 *Mittagessen* (lunch) approx. between midday and 2 pm. Traditionally lunch consists of a hot dish and is the most important meal of the day. Offices and shops often close while lunch is taken at home, in a restaurant or canteen. It usually consists of two or three courses:
– starter
– main course
– dessert

3 *Abendessen* (dinner)/*Vesper* (cold evening meal in southern Germany) between 6 and 9.30 pm. This either consists of a light hot meal or a cold meal such as slices of bread with cold meat, cheese and salad.

 .1 On arrival

I'd like to book a table for seven o'clock, please	Kann ich einen Tisch für sieben Uhr reservieren lassen? *kann ikh ainen tish fuer zeeben ooer rezerveeren lassen?*
I'd like a table for two, please	Bitte einen Tisch für zwei Personen *bitter ainen tish fuer tsvai perzoanen*
We've/we haven't booked	Wir haben (nicht) reserviert *veer harben (nikht) rezerveert*
Is the restaurant open yet?	Hat die Küche schon geöffnet? *hat dee kuekher shoan goooffnet?*
What time does the restaurant open/close?	Wann öffnet/schliesst die Küche? *vann oeffnet/shleest dee kuekher?*
Can we wait for a table?	Können wir auf einen Tisch warten? *koennen veer owf ainen tish varten?*
Do we have to wait long?	Müssen wir lange warten? *muessen veer langer varten?*

Haben Sie reserviert?	Do you have a reservation?
Unter welchem Namen?	What name, please?
Hierher bitte	This way, please
Dieser Tisch ist reserviert	This table is reserved
In einer Viertelstunde wird ein Tisch frei	We'll have a table free in fifteen minutes
Möchten Sie solange (an der Bar) warten?	Would you like to wait (at the bar)?

Is this seat taken?	Ist dieser Platz frei? *ist deezer plats frai?*
Could we sit here/there?	Können wir uns hierher/dahin setzen? *koennen veer oons heerhair/darhin zetsen?*
Can we sit by the window?	Können wir uns ans Fenster setzen? *koennen veer oons ans fenster zetsen?*

Can we eat outside?	Können wir auch draussen essen?
	koennen veer owkh drowsen essen?
Do you have another chair for us?	Könnten Sie uns noch einen Stuhl bringen?
	koennten zee oons nokh ainen shtool bringen?
Do you have a highchair?	Könnten Sie uns einen Kinderstuhl bringen?
	koennten zee oons ainen kindershtool bringen?
Is there a socket for this bottle-warmer?	Gibt es für diesen Flaschenwärmer eine Steckdose?
	gipt es fuer deezen flashen vayrmerr ainer shtekdozer?
Could you warm up this bottle/jar for me?	Könnten Sie mir dieses Fläschchen/Gläschen aufwärmen?
	koennten zee meer deezez fleshkhen/glayzkhen owfvermen?
Not too hot, please	Nicht zu heiss bitte
	nikht tsoo haiss bitter
Is there somewhere I can change the baby's nappy?	Gibt es hier einen Raum, wo ich das Baby wickeln kann?
	gipt ez heer ainen rowm vo ikh dass bayby vikkeln kann?
Where are the toilets?	Wo ist die Toilette?
	vo ist dee twaletter?

4 .2 Ordering

Waiter!	Herr Ober!
	herr oaber!
Madam!	Bedienung!
	bedeenoong!
Sir!	Bitte!
	bitter!
We'd like something to eat/a drink	Wir möchten gern etwas essen/trinken
	veer moekhten gayrn etvass essen/trinken
Could I have a quick meal?	Könnte ich schnell etwas essen?
	koennter ikh shnell etvass essen?
We don't have much time	Wir haben wenig Zeit
	veer harben vaynikh tsait
We'd like to have a drink first	Wir möchten erst noch etwas trinken
	veer moekhten ayrst nokh etvass trinken
Could we see the menu/wine list, please?	Wir hätten gern die Speisekarte/Weinkarte/(Getränkekarte)
	veer hetten gayrn dee spaizer karter/vain karter(gertrenker karte)
Do you have a menu in English?	Haben Sie eine Speisekarte in Englisch?
	harben zee ainer shpayzer karter in english?
Do you have a dish of the day?	Haben Sie ein Tagesmenü/Touristenmenü?
	harben zee ain targes menyoo/toorissten menyoo?
We haven't made a choice yet	Wir haben noch nicht gewählt
	veer harben nokh nikht gevaylt
What do you recommend?	Was können Sie uns empfehlen?
	vass koennen zee oons empfaylen?

What are the specialities of the region/the house?	Welches sind die Spezialitäten dieser Gegend/des Hauses?
	velkhes zint dee shpetseeali tayten deezer gegent/dez howzez?
I like strawberries/olives	Ich liebe Erdbeeren/Oliven
	ikh leeber ertbeeren/olleeven
I don't like meat/fish/...	Ich mag kein Fleisch/keinen Fisch
	ikh mark kain flaish/kainen fish
What's this?	Was ist das?
	vass ist dass?
Does it have...in it?	Ist das mit...?
	ist dass mit...?
What does it taste like?	Womit kann man das vergleichen?
	vo-mitt kann mann dass fairglaikhen?
Is this a hot or a cold dish?	Ist dieses Gericht warm oder kalt?
	ist deezes gerikht varm oader kalt?
Is this sweet?	Ist es eine Süßspeise?
	ist ez ainer suess shpaizer?
Is this spicy?	Ist es pikant/scharf?
	ist es peekant/sharf?
Do you have anything else, please?	Haben Sie vielleicht etwas anderes?
	harben zee feelaihkt etvass anderez?
I'm on a salt-free diet	Ich darf kein Salz essen
	ikh darf kain zalts essen
I can't eat pork	Ich darf kein Schweinefleisch essen
	ikh darf kain shvainer flaish essen
– sugar	Ich darf keinen Zucker essen
	ikh darf kainen tsooker essen
– fatty foods	Ich darf kein Fett essen
	ikh darf kain fet essen
– (hot) spices	Ich darf keine scharfen Gewürze essen
	ikh darf kainer sharfen gevuertser essen
I'll/we'll have what those people are having	Ich möchte/wir möchten gern dasselbe wie die Leute da
	ikh moekhter/veer moekhten gayrn dass selber vee dee loyter dar
I'd like...	Ich möchte...
	ikh moekhter...
We're not having a starter	Wir nehmen keine Vorspeise
	veer naymen kainer for shpaizer

Möchten Sie essen/speisen?	Would you like to eat?
Haben Sie schon gewählt?	Have you decided?
Möchten Sie eine Nachspeise?	Would you like a dessert?
Was darf es sein?	What would you like?
Guten Appetit!	Enjoy your meal
Darf/Dürfte ich jetzt abrechnen?	May I ask you to settle the bill, please?

The child will share____ what we're having	Das Kind isst etwas von unserem Menü mit
dass kint ist etvass fon oonzerem menyoo mit
Could I have some ____ more bread, please?	Noch etwas Brot bitte
nokh etvass broat bitter
– a bottle of water/wine____	Noch eine Flasche (Mineral)wasser/Wein bitte
nokh ainer flasher (minerarl)vasser/vain bitter
– another helping of... ____	Noch eine Portion....bitte
nokh ainer portseeoan...bitter
– some salt and pepper____	Würden Sie bitte Salz und Pfeffer bringen?
vuerden zee bitter zalts unt pfeffer bringen?
– a napkin ____	Würden Sie bitte eine Serviette bringen?
vuerden zee bitter ainer zerviyetter bringen?
– a spoon____	Würden Sie bitte einen Löffel bringen?
vuerden zee bitter ainen loeffel bringen?
– an ashtray ____	Würden Sie bitte einen Aschenbecher bringen?
vuerden zee bitter ainen ashen bekher bringen?
– some matches____	Würden Sie bitte Streichhölzer bringen?
vuerden zee bitter shtraikh hoeltser bringen?
– a glass of water ____	Würden Sie bitte ein Glas Wasser bringen?
vuerden zee bitter ain glars vasser bringen?
– a straw (for the child) ____	Würden Sie bitte (für das Kind) einen Trinkhalm bringen?
vuerden zee bitter (fuer dass kint) ainen trinkhalm bringen?
Enjoy your meal!____	Guten Appetit!
gooten appeteet!
You too! ____	Danke, gleichfalls
dunker, glaikhfals
Cheers! ____	Prost/zum Wohl!
prrosst/tsoom voal!
The next round's on me ____	Die nächste Runde gebe ich (aus)
dee nexter roonder gayber ikh (ows)
Could we have a doggy____ bag, please?	Dürfen wir die Reste mitnehmen?
duerfen veer dee rester mitnaymen?

4.3 The bill

See also 8.2 Settling the bill

How much is this dish? ____	Wieviel kostet dieses Gericht?
veefeel kostet deezes gerikht?
Could I have the bill, ____ please?	Die Rechnung bitte
dee rekhnoong bitter
All together ____	Alles zusammen
alles tsoozammen
Everyone pays separately__	Getrennt zahlen
getrennt tsarlen

Could we have the menu again, please?	Dürften wir die Karte noch mal sehen? *duerften veer dee karter nokh marl zayhen?*
The...is not on the bill	Der/die/das...steht nicht auf der Rechnung *der/dee/dass...shtayt nikht owf dayr rekhnoong*

4 .4 Complaints

It's taking a very long time	Das dauert aber lange *dass dowert arber langer*
We've been here an hour already	Wir sitzen hier schon seit einer Stunde *veer zitsen heer shoan zait ainer shtoonder*
This must be a mistake	Das muss ein Irrtum sein *dass muss ain eartoom zain*
This is not what I ordered	Das habe ich nicht bestellt *dass harber ikh nikht beshtellt*
I ordered...	Ich habe um...gebeten *ikh harber oom...gebayten*
There's a dish missing	Es fehlt ein Gericht *ez faylt ain gerikht*
This is broken/not clean	Das ist kaputt/nicht sauber *dass ist kapoott/nikht zowber*
The food's cold	Das Essen ist kalt *dass essen ist kalt*
– not fresh	Das Essen ist nicht frisch *dass essen ist nikht frish*
– too salty/sweet/spicy	Das Essen ist versalzen/zu süss/scharf *dass essen ist fairzaltsen/tsoo zuess/sharf*
The meat's not done	Das Fleisch ist nicht gar *dass flaish ist nikht garr*
– overdone	Das Fleisch ist zu sehr durchgebraten *dass flaish ist tsoo zayr doorkh gebrarten*
– tough	Das Fleisch ist zäh *dass flaish ist tsay*
– off	Das Fleisch ist verdorben *dass flaish ist fairdorben*
Could I have something else instead of this?	Können Sie mir hierfür etwas anderes bringen? *koennen zee meer heerfuerr etvass anderez bringen?*
The bill/this amount is not right	Die Rechnung/dieser Betrag stimmt nicht *dee rekhnoong/deezer betrark shtimmt nikht*
We didn't have this	Das haben wir nicht gehabt *dass harben veer nihkt gehapt*
There's no paper in the toilet	Auf der Toilette ist kein Toilettenpapier *owf der twaletter ist kain twaletten papeer*
Do you have a complaints book?	haben Sie ein Beschwerdebuch *harben zee ain beshverder bookh?*
Will you call the manager, please?	Würden Sie bitte den Chef rufen? *vuerden zee bitter den shef roofen?*

.5 Paying a compliment

That was a wonderful meal	Wir haben herrlich gegessen *veer harben hairlikh gegessen*
The food was excellent	Es hat uns ausgezeichnet geschmeckt *ez hat oons owsge tsaikhnet geshmekt*
The...in particular was delicious	Vor allem der/die/das...war hervorragend *for allem dayr/dee/dass...var hair for rargent*

.6 The menu

Bedienung einschliesslich service included	Getränke (karte) beverages/list of beverages (café) or wine list (restaurant)	Suppen soups
Beilagen side-dishes		Tagesmenü menu of the day
Erfrischungsgetränke refreshment drinks	Happen snack	Tagesteller dish of the day
Fisch fish	Hauptgerichte main courses	Torten gateau/flan (with fruit)
Frühstück breakfast	Köstlichkeiten delicacies	
Gebäck biscuits, pastries, buns, tarts, tartlets	Kuchen cake(s)	Vorspeisen starters
	Meeresfrüchte seafood	Weine wines
Gedeck set meal/place	Nachspeisen desserts	Weinkarte wine list
Gerichte dishes	Spezialitäten specialities	Zwischengerichte entrée/snack

.7 Alphabetical list of drinks and dishes

Aal eel	-frühstück bacon and potato omelette	Bratkartoffeln fried potatoes
Apfel apple	Beeren berries	Brause pop/lemonade
Äpfel im Schlafrock baked apples in puff pastry	Birne pears	Bries(chen), Briesel dish containing sweetbreads of animals (mostly calves)
Apfelsine orange	Bismarckhering Bismarck herring (filleted pickled herring)	
Aspik aspic		Brombeere blackberry
Aufschnitt sliced cold meat or (rarer) cheese	Blaubeere blueberry	Brot bread
Austern oysters	Blaukraut red cabbage	Brötchen bread rolls
Bauern- farmer's/rustic	Bohnen (grüne, grosse) green beans	Brühe clear soup/stock
-brot coarse rye bread	Braten roast	Brust breast

Bündner Fleisch
smoked ham from
  the region of
  Graubünden in
  Switzerland

Butt
flounder/butt

Butter
butter

Chicoree
chicory

Curry
curry

Dampfnudeln
sweet yeast
  dumpling cooked in
  milk and sugar

Dattel
date

Dörr-
dried

Dorsch
cod

Eierkuchen (dünn)
(thin) pancakes

Eierstich
egg based ingredient
  of some soups

Eintopf
stew

Eisbecher
sundae(s)

Eisbombe
ice cream cake

Endivie
endive

Ente
duck

Erbsen
peas

Erdbeere
strawberry

Essig
vinegar

Fadennudeln
vermicelli

Feige
fig

Filetsteak
fillet steak

Fisch
fish

Fisolen
green beans

Fleisch
meat

Flusskrebs
crayfish

Frikassee (Hühner-)
(chicken) fricassee

Frittatensuppe
  soup containing
  strips of pancake

Frühlingsrolle
spring rolls

Gänseleber
goose liver

Garnele
shrimp

gebraten
fried

gedünstet
braised

Geflügel
poultry

gefüllt
filled/stuffed

gekocht
boiled

Gelee
jelly

Gemüse
vegetables

geräuchert
smoked

Geschnetzeltes
meat cut into strips
  stewed to produce
  a thick sauce

Geselchtes
salted and smoked
  meat

gespickt
larded/fried meat
  with strips of bacon

getrocknet
dried

gewürzt
seasoned

Glühwein
mulled wine

Grog
grog

Gulasch
goulash

Gurke (saure-)
(pickled) gherkins

Hähnchen/Hühnchen
chicken

Hase
hare

Haselnuss
hazelnut

Hasenpfeffer
jugged hare

Hering
herring

Heurige(r)
new wine

Himbeere
raspberry

Hirn
brains

Hirsch
venison

Hummer
lobster

Ingwer
ginger

Jause
snack

Johannisbeere
blackcurrant/redcurrant

Kalb
calf

Kaldaunen/Kutteln
tripe

Kaltschale
cold sweet soup

Kaninchen
rabbit

Karfiol
cauliflower

Karotten
carrots

Karpfen
carp

Kartoffel
potato

Kartoffelpuffer
potato fritter

Käse
cheese

Kekse
biscuits

Keule
leg

Kirsche
cherry

Klösse (Kartoffel-,
Semmel-)
dumplings (potato,
bread)

Knoblauch
garlic

Knödel
dumplings

Knusprig
crisp/crunchy
Kochschinken
boiled ham
Kompott
stewed fruit/compote
Konfitüre
jam
Korn
corn/corn schnapps
Krabbe
crab
Krapfen
doughnut
Kräuter-
herbal
Labskaus
stew made of meat,
  fish and mashed
  potato
Lachs
salmon
Languste
crayfish
Lauch
leek
Lebkuchen
gingerbread
Likör
liqueur
Mandel
almond
Marille
apricot
mariniert
marinated
Marone
chestnut
Maultaschen
filled pasta squares
Meerrettich
horseradish
Melone
melon
Mett
minced pork/beef
Milch
milk
Muscheln
mussels
Nockerl
little dumplings
Nougat
nougat

Obst (je nach
  Jahreszeit/Saison)
fruit (of the season)
Obstkuchen
fruitcake
Obstler
fruit schnapps
Ochsenschwanz
oxtail
Öl
oil
Orange
orange
Palatschinken
stuffed pancake
Pampelmuse
grapefruit
Pastete
paté
Petersilie
parsley
Pfannkuchen
pancake
Pfeffer
pepper
Pfifferling
chanterelle
Pfirsich
peach
Pflaume
plum
Pilze
mushrooms
Platte
plate
Plätzchen
biscuit/cookie
Pommes frites
French fries
Porree
leek
Preßsack
a type of cold meat
Pute
turkey
Quark
(soft) curd cheese
Radieschen
radish
Rahm
cream
Räucherschinken
smoked ham
Rebhuhn
partridge

Reh
deer
Reibekuchen
potato waffle
Reis
rice
Remoulade
remoulade
resch (rösch)
crisp/crusty
Rinder-
beef
Rinderfilet
beef fillet
Rindfleisch
beef
Rippe
rib
roh
raw
Rosenkohl
Brussels sprouts
Rosine
raisin
Rostbraten
roast
Röstkartoffeln
fried potatoes
rote Beete
beetroot
Rührei
scrambled eggs
Rumpsteak
rump steak
Sachertorte
a rich chocolate cake
Saft
juice
Sahne
cream
Salat (gemischt)
salad (mixed)
Salzkartoffeln
boiled potatoes
Sauerkraut
sauerkraut/pickled
  cabbage
Schaum-
frothy
Schildkrötensuppe
turtle soup
Schinken
ham
Schlagobers
whipped cream

Schmalz
lard
Schmarren
pancake cut up into
  small pieces
Schnecken
escargots
Schnittchen (Appe-
tit)
canapé
Schnittlauch
chives
Schorle
wine and soda water
  mix
Schweinefleisch
pork
Schweinelendchen
small pieces of pork
loin
Sekt
sparkling wine
Sellerie
celery
Semmel
bread roll
Senf
mustard
Sosse
gravy/sauce
Spanferkel
whole pig roasted
  over an open fire
Spargel
asparagus
Spätzle
spaetzle (type of
  pasta)

Speiseeis
ice-cream
Spinat
spinach
Steinpilz
type of mushroom
  (*Boletus edulis*)
Strammer Max
open sandwich of
  boiled ham and
  fried egg
Strudel
strudel
Süßspeise
sweet dish
Teig (in Öl gebacken)
pastry, batter (baked
  in oil)
Thunfisch
tuna
Tintenfisch
cuttlefish/squid
Topfen
soft curd cheese
Traube
grape
Truthahn
turkey
Tunke
sauce/gravy
Vesper
a break for
  eating/cold evening
  meal
Wachtel
quail
Wald-
forest

Walnuss
walnut
Wein (trocken/mild)
wine (dry/mild)
Wein (süss/
Spätlese/Eiswein)
wine (sweet/late
  vintage/sweet wine
  made from grapes
  which have been
  exposed to frost)
Wein (Süsswein/
Südwein)
wine (dessert
  wine/
  Mediterranean wine)
Weinbrand
brandy
Weisswurst
veal sausage
Wels
catfish
Würstchen
sausage
Zitrone
lemon
Zunge
tongue
Zwiebel
onion

On the road

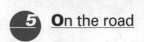

5 On the road

5.1 Asking for directions

Excuse me, could I ask you something? — Verzeihung, dürfte ich Sie etwas fragen?
fair tsaioong, duerfter ikh zee etvass frargen?

I've lost my way — Ich habe mich verlaufen/(with car)mich verfahren
ikh harber mikh fairlowfen/mikh fairfahren

Is there a(n)... around here? — Wissen Sie, wo hier in der Nähe ein(e)... ist?
vissen zee, vo heer in dayr nayher ain(er)... ist?

Is this the way to...? — Ist dies die Strasse nach...?
ist dees dee shtrasser nakh...?

Could you tell me how to get to the... (name of place) by car/on foot? — Können Sie mir sagen, wie ich nach... (name of the place) fahren/gehen muss?
koenen zee meer zargen, vee ikh nakh ... fahren/gayhen muss?

What's the quickest way to...? — Wie komme ich am schnellsten nach...?
vee kommer ikh am shnellsten nakh...?

How many kilometres is it to...? — Wieviel Kilometer sind es noch bis...?
veefeel kilomayter zint ez nokh biss...?

Could you point it out on the map? — Können Sie es mir auf der Karte zeigen?
koennen zee ez meer owf dayr karter tsaigen?

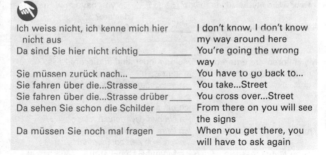

Ich weiss nicht, ich kenne mich hier nicht aus	I don't know, I don't know my way around here
Da sind Sie hier nicht richtig	You're going the wrong way
Sie müssen zurück nach...	You have to go back to...
Sie fahren über die...Strasse	You take...Street
Sie fahren über die...Strasse drüber	You cross over...Street
Da sehen Sie schon die Schilder	From there on you will see the signs
Da müssen Sie noch mal fragen	When you get there, you will have to ask again

geradeaus straight	überqueren cross	der Fluss the river
nach links/links abbiegen left/turn left	die Kreuzung the intersection	die Brücke the bridge
nach rechts/rechts abbiegen right/turn right	die Strasse the street	die (Bahn)schranken the level crossing/ the boomgates
abbiegen turn	die (Verkehrs)ampel the traffic light	das Schild Richtung ... the sign pointing to ...
folgen follow	das Gebäude the building	der Pfeil the arrow
	an der Ecke at the corner	

On the road

45

5.2 Customs

● **Border documents** Germany: valid passport. For car and motorbike: valid UK driving licence and registration document, insurance document, green card, UK registration plate, country identification sticker on the back of the car, First Aid kit containing sterile gloves. Caravan: must be entered on the green card, country identification sticker must be visible. A warning triangle, headlight convertors and extra headlamp bulbs must be carried.
Import and export specifications:
Foreign currency: no restrictions
With the single European Market, travellers are only subject to selective spot checks. There is no restriction, either by quantity or value, on goods purchased by travellers in another EC country provided they are for their own personal use. However, guidelines have been published. As these are subject to change you are advised to contact your travel agent, customs or the Embassy for further details before travelling.

Ihren Pass bitte _____	Your passport, please
Die grüne Karte bitte _____	Your green card, please
Ihre Fahrzeugpapiere bitte _____	Your vehicle documents, please
Ihr Visum bitte _____	Your visa, please
Wohin fahren Sie? _____	Where are you heading?
Wie lange bleiben Sie/halten Sie sich dort auf? _____	How long are you planning to stay?
Haben Sie etwas zu verzollen? _____	Do you have anything to declare?
Würden Sie dies bitte öffnen? _____	Open this, please

My children are entered ___ on this passport	Meine Kinder sind in diesem Pass eingetragen *mainer kinder zint in deezem parss ain getrargen*
I'm travelling through _____	Ich bin auf der Durchreise *ikh bin owf dayr doorkh raizer*
I'm going on holiday to... __	*Ich fahre in den Urlaub nach...* *ikh fahrer in den oorlowp nakh...*
I'm on a business trip _____	Ich bin auf Geschäftsreise *ikh bin owf geshefts raizer*
I don't know how long I'll be staying yet	Ich weiss noch nicht, wie lange ich bleibe *ikh vaiss nokh nikht, vee langer ikh blaiber*
I'll be staying here for _____ a weekend	Ich bleibe hier übers Wochenende *ikh blaiber heer uebers vokhen ender*
– for a few days _____	Ich bleibe hier ein paar Tage *ikh blaiber heer ain par targer*
– for a week_____	Ich bleibe hier eine Woche *ikh blaiber heer ainer vokher*
– for two weeks _____	Ich bleibe hier zwei Wochen *ikh blaiber heer tsvai vokhen*
I've got nothing to_____ declare	Ich habe nichts zu verzollen *ikh harber nikhts tsoo fairtsollen*

I've got...with me	Ich habe ... mit
	ikh harber ... mit
– a carton of cigarettes	Ich habe eine Stange Zigaretten
	ikh harber ainer shtanger tseegaretten
– a bottle of...	Ich habe eine Flasche...
	ikh harber ainer flusher...
– some souvenirs	Ich habe ein paar Andenken
	ikh harber ain par andenken
These are personal effects	Das sind persönliche Sachen
	dass zint perzoenlikher zakhen
These are not new	Diese Sachen sind nicht neu
	deezer zakhen zint nikht noy
Here's the receipt	Hier ist der (Kassen)zettel
	heer ist dayr (kassen)tsettel
This is for private use	Das ist für den eigenen Gebrauch
	dass ist fuer dayn aigenen gebrowkh
How much import duty do I have to pay?	Wieviel Einfuhrzoll muss ich zahlen?
	veefeel ainfoor tsoll muss ikh tsarlen?
Can I go now?	Darf ich jetzt gehen?
	darf ikh yetst gayhen?
Porter!	Gepäckträger!
	gepeck trayger!
Could you take this luggage to...?	Würden Sie dieses Gepäck zu/in... bringen?
	vuerden zee deezes gepek tsoo/in... bringen?

5 .3 Luggage

How much do I owe you?	Wieviel bekommen Sie von mir?
	veefeel bekommen zee fon meer?
Where can I find a luggage trolley?	Wo kann ich eine Gepäckkarre finden?
	vo kann ikh ainer gepek karrer finden?
Could you store this luggage for me?	Kann ich dieses Gepäck zur Aufbewahrung abgeben?
	kann ikh deezes gepek tsoor owfbevahrung apgayben?
Where are the luggage lockers?	Wo sind die Schliessfächer?
	vo zint dee shleess fekher?
I can't get the locker open	Ich bekomme das Schliessfach nicht auf
	ikh bekommer dass shleessfakh nikht owf
How much is it per item per day?	Wieviel kostet es je Stück pro Tag?
	veefeel kostet es yay shtuek pro tark?
This is not my bag/ suitcase	Das ist nicht meine Tasche/mein Koffer
	dass ist nikht mainer tasher/main koffer
There's one item/bag/ suitcase missing still	Es fehlt noch ein Stück/eine Tasche/ein Koffer
	ez faylt nokh ain shtuek/ayner tasher/ain koffer
My suitcase is damaged	Mein Koffer ist beschädigt
	main koffer ist beshaydikt

abbiegen
turn
Anlieger frei
residents only
Auffahrt
slip road/approach
  to house
Auflieger schwenkt
  aus
trailer may swing
  out
Ausfahrt
exit
Autobahndreieck
motorway merging
  point
Baustelle
road works ahead
bei Nässe/Glätte
in wet -/icy
  conditions
Durchgangsverkehr
  (verboten)
(no) throughway
Einbahnstrasse
one way street
Einfahrt
entry/access
Ende der Autobahn
end of motorway
Frostaufbrüche
frost damage
Gefahr
danger
gefährlich
dangerous
Gegenverkehr
oncoming traffic

gesperrt (für alle
  Fahrzeuge)
closed (for all
  vehicles)
Glatteis
ice on road
Kurve(nreiche
  Strecke)
bend/dangerous
  bends
Licht einschalten/
  ausschalten
switch on lights/end
needs for lights
LKW
heavy goods vehicle
Naturschutzgebiet
nature reserve
Nebel
beware fog
Parkscheibe
parking disk
PKW
motorcar
Radfahrer kreuzen
cyclists crossing
Rasthof-stätte
services
Rastplatz bitte
  sauberhalten
please keep picnic
  area tidy
Rollsplit
loose chippings
Schleudergefahr
danger of skidding
Seitenstreifen nicht
  befahrbar
soft verges

Seitenwind
crosswind
Spurrillen
irregular road
  surface
Standstreifen
hard shoulder
Starkes Gefälle
steep hill
Stau
traffic jam
Stauwarnanlage
hazard lights
Steinschlag
falling stones
Talbrücke
bridge over a valley
Überholverbot
no overtaking
Umleitung
diversion
Unbeschränkter
  Bahnübergang
unguarded level
  crossing/dangerous
  crossing
Verengte Fahrbahn
narrow lane
Vorfahrt beachten
give way
Vorfahrtsstrasse
major road
Wasserschutzgebiet
protected reservoir
  area
zurückschalten
to change back

5 .5 The car

See the diagram on page 51.

● **Particular traffic regulations:**
Maximum speed for cars:
130 km/h recommended on motorways
90 km/h outside town centres
50 km/h in town centres
Give way: all traffic from the right has right of way, including slow
  vehicles, except for major roads and other regulating traffic signs. At
  roundabouts the traffic already on the roundabout has priority.
Seat belts: compulsory in the front and the back

5 .6 The petrol station

● **The petrol prices in Germany**, Austria and Switzerland are
comparable to those in the UK.

How many kilometres to the next petrol station, please?	Wieviel Kilometer sind es bis zur nächsten Tankstelle? *veefeel kilomayter zint ez biss tsoor nexten tankshteller?*
I would like...litres of..., please	Ich möchte ... Liter *ikh moekhter ... liter*
– super	Ich möchte ... Liter Super(benzin) *ikh moehkter ... liter zooper(bentseen)*
– leaded	Ich möchte ... Liter normal(es Bezin) *ikh moekhter ... liter normarl(ez bentseen)*
– unleaded	Ich möchte ... Liter bleifrei(es Benzin) *ikh moekhter ... liter blaifrai(ez bentseen)*
– diesel	Ich möchte ... Liter Diesel *ikh moekhter ... liter deezel*
I would like... Marks/Schilling/ Franks worth of petrol, please	Ich möchte für ... Mark/Schilling/Franken (Auto)gas *ikh moekhter fuer ... mark/shilling/franken (owto)gass*
Fill her up, please	Voll bitte *foll bitter*
Could you check...?	Würden Sie bitte...kontrollieren? *vuerden zee bitter...kontrolleeren?*
– the oil level	Kontrollieren Sie bitte den Ölstand *kontrolleeren zee bitter dayn oelshtant*
– the tyre pressure	Kontrollieren Sie bitte den Reifendruck *kontrolleeren zee bitter dayn raifendrukk*
Could you change the oil, please?	Wechseln Sie bitte das Öl *vekhseln zee bitter dass oel*
Could you clean the windows/the windscreen, please?	Reinigen Sie bitte die Windschutzscheibe *rainigen zee bitter dee vint shoots shaiber*
Could you give the car a wash, please?	Kann ich hier mein Auto waschen lassen? *kann ikh main owto heer vashen lassen?*

On the road

The parts of a car
(the diagram shows the numbered parts)

1	battery	der Akku/die Batterie	*dayr akoo/batteree*
2	rear light	das Rücklicht	*dass ruekleekht*
3	rear-view mirror	der Rückspiegel	*dayr ruekshpeegell*
	reversing light	der Rückfahrscheinwerfer	*dayr ruckfahrshaynverfer*
4	aerial	die Antenne	*dee antennar*
	car radio	das Autoradio	*dass owtorardiyoo*
5	petrol tank	der Benzintank	*dayr bentseentank*
	inside mirror	der Innenspiegel	*dayr innenshpeegel*
6	sparking plugs	die Zündkerze(n)	*dee tsuentkairtsen*
	fuel filter/pump	das Treibstofffilter/die Triebstoffpumpe	*dass traipshtofffilter/dee traipshtoffpoomper*
7	wing mirror	der Aussenspiegel	*dayr owsenshpeegel*
8	bumper	die Stoßstange	*dee shtoass shtanger*
	carburettor	der Vergaser	*dayr fairgarzer*
	crankcase	das Kurbelgehäuse	*dass koorbellgehoyzer*
	cylinder	der Zylinder	*dayr tsilinder*
	ignition	die Zündung	*dee tsuendoong*
	warning light	die Kontrollampe	*dee kontroal lamper*
	dynamo	der Dynamo	*dayr deenamo*
	accelerator	das Gaspedal	*dass gas pedarl*
	handbrake	die Handbremse	*dee hantbremzer*
	valve	das Ventil	*dass venteel*
9	silencer	der Auspufftopf	*dayr owspufftopf*
10	boot	der Kofferraum	*dayr kofferrowm*
11	headlight	der Scheinwerfer	*dayr shaynverfer*
	crank shaft	die Kurbelwelle	*dee koorbelveller*
12	air filter	das Luftfilter	*dass looftfilter*
	fog lamp	die Nebelleuchte	*dee naybel loykhter*
13	engine block	der Motorblock	*dayr moatorblock*
	camshaft	die Nockenwelle	*dee nokkenveller*
	oil filter/pump	das Ölfilter/dieÖlpumpe	*dass oelfilter/dee oelpoomper*
	dipstick	der Ölstandstab	*dayr oelshtuntshtarp*
	pedal	das Pedal	*dass pedarl*
14	door	die Wagentür	*dee vargentuer*
15	radiator	der Kühler	*dayr kuehler*
16	brake disc	die Bremsscheibe	*dee bremzshayber*
	spare wheel	das Ersatzrad	*dass erzatsrart*
17	indicator	der Blinker	*dayr blinker*
18	windscreen wiper	der Scheibenwischer	*dayr shaibenvisher*
19	shock absorbers	der Stossdämpfer	*dayr shtossdempfer*
	sunroof	das Schiebdach	*dass sheebedakh*
	spoiler	der Spoiler	*dayr shpoyler*
	starter motor	der Startmotor	*dayr shtartmoator*
20	steering column	die Lenksäule	*dee lenkzoyler*
21	exhaust pipe	das Auspuffrohr	*dass owspoofrohr*
22	seat belt	der Sicherheitsgurt	*dayr zikherhaitsgoort*
	fan	der Ventilator	*dayr venteelator*
23	distributor cables	das Verteilerkabel	*dass fertailerkarbel*
24	gear lever	der Schalthebel	*dayr shalt-haybel*

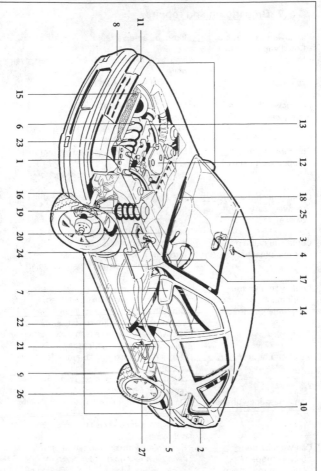

25 windscreen	die Windschutzscheibe	*dee vintshootsshaiber*
water pump	die Wasserpumpe	*dee vasserpoomper*
26 wheel	das Rad	*dass rart*
27 hubcap	die Radkappe	*dee rartkapper*
piston	der Kolben	*dayr kolben*

I'm having car trouble. Could you give me a hand?	Ich habe eine Panne. Können Sie mir helfen?
	ikh harber ainer panner. koennen zee meer helfen?
I've run out of petrol	Ich habe kein Benzin mehr
	ikh harber kain bentseen mayr
I've locked the keys in the car	Ich habe die Schlüssel im Auto steckenlassen
	ikh harber dee shluessel im owto shtekken lassen
The car/motorbike/ moped won't start	Das Auto/Motorrad/Moped springt nicht an
	dass owto/moator rat/moapet shprinkt nikht an
Could you contact the recovery service for me, please?	Könnten Sie für mich die Pannenhilfe benachrichtigen?
	koennten zee fuer mikh dee pannen hilfer benakh rikhtigen?
Could you call a garage for me, please?	Könnten Sie für mich eine Werkstatt anrufen?
	koennten zee fuer mikh ainer vairkshtatt anroofen?
Could you give me a lift to...?	Darf ich mit Ihnen nach...mitfahren?
	darf ikh mit eenen nakh...mitfahren?
– a garage/into town?	Darf ich mit Ihnen bis zu einer Werkstatt/in die Stadt mitfahren?
	darf ikh mit eenen biss tsoo ainer verkshtatt/in dee shtatt mit fahren?
– a phone booth?	Darf ich mit Ihnen bis zu einer Telefonzelle mitfahren?
	darf ikh mit eenen biss tsoo ainer tellefoan tseller mit fahren?
– an emergency phone?	Darf ich mit Ihnen bis zu einer Rufsäule mitfahren?
	darf ikh mit eenen biss tsoo ainer roofzoyler mit fahren?
Can we take my bicycle/moped?	Kann mein Fahrrad/Moped auch mit?
	kann main fahr rat/moapet owkh mit?
Could you tow me to a garage?	Könnten Sie mich zu einer Werkstatt (ab)schleppen?
	koennten zee mikh tsoo ainer verkshtatt (ap)shleppen?
There's probably something wrong with...(See pages 51–52)	Wahrscheinlich ist mit dem/der/den...etwas nicht in Ordnung
	varshainlikh ist mit daym/dayr/dayn...etvass nikht in ordnoong
Can you fix it?	Können Sie es reparieren?
	koennen zee es repareeren?
Could you fix my tyre?	Können Sie den Reifen flicken?
	koennen zee dayn raifen flikken?
Could you change this wheel?	Können Sie das Rad wechseln?
	koennen zee dass rart vekhzeln?

Can you fix it so it'll get me to...?	Können Sie es soweit reparieren, dass ich damit nach ... fahren kann?
	koennen zee es zovait repareeren dass ikh darmit nakh ... fahren kann?
Which garage can help me?	Welche Werkstatt kann mir denn dann helfen?
	velkher verkshtatt kann meer denn dann helfen?
When will my car/bicycle be ready?	Wann ist mein Auto/Fahrrad fertig?
	vann ist main owto/fahr rart fairtikh?
Can I wait for it here?	Kann ich hier darauf warten?
	kann ikh heer darrowf varten?
How much will it cost?	Wieviel wird es kosten?
	veefeel virt es kosten?
Could you itemise the bill?	Können Sie die Rechnung spezifizieren?
	koennen zee dee rekhnoong shpetsi fitseeren?
Can I have a receipt for the insurance?	Ich hätte gern eine Quittung für die Versicherung
	ikh hetter gayrn ainer kvittoong fuer dee fairzikheroong

5 .8 The bicycle/moped

See the diagram on page 55.

● **Cycle paths** are common in towns and cities and their use is strongly recommended. Bikes can usually be hired at tourist centres. The maximum speed for mopeds is 40 km/h both inside and outside town centres. Crash helmets are compulsory.

Ich habe keine Ersatzteile für Ihren Wagen/Ihr Fahrrad	I don't have parts for your car/bicycle
Ich muss die Ersatzteile irgendwo anders besorgen	I have to get the parts from somewhere else
Ich muss die Ersatzteile bestellen	I have to order the parts
Das dauert einen halben Tag	That'll take half a day
Das dauert einen Tag	That'll take a day
Das dauert ein paar Tage	That'll take a few days
Das dauert eine Woche	That'll take a week
Ihr Auto ist schrottreif	Your car is a write-off
Hier ist nichts mehr zu machen	It can't be repaired
Das Auto/Motorrad/Moped/ Fahrrad ist um...Uhr fertig	The car/motor bike/moped/bicycle will be ready at...o'clock

The parts of a bicycle
(the diagram shows the numbered parts)

1 rear lamp	das Rücklicht	*dass rueklikht*
2 rear wheel	das Hinterrad	*dass hinterrart*
3 (luggage) carrier	der Gepäckträger	*dayr gepektrayger*
4 bicycle fork	das Steuer(kopf)rohr	*dass shtoyerkopfrohr*
5 bell	die Klingel	*dee klingel*
inner tube	der Schlauch	*dayr shlowkh*
tyre	der Reifen	*dayr raifen*
6 crank	die Kurbel	*dee koorbel*
7 gear change	der Umwerfer	*dayr oomverfer*
wire	das Kabel	*dass karbel*
dynamo	der Dynamo	*dayr deenamo*
bicycle trailer	der Fahrradanhänger	*dayr fahrrartanhenger*
frame	der Rahmen	*dayr rarmen*
8 dress guard	der Kleiderschutz	*dayr klaidershoots*
9 chain	die Kette	*dee ketter*
chain guard	der Kettenschutz	*dayr kettenshoots*
chain lock	das Kettenschloss	*dass kettenshloss*
milometer	der Kilometerzähler	*dayr keelomaytertsayler*
child's seat	der Kindersitz	*dayr kinderzits*
10 headlamp	der Scheinwerfer	*dayr shainverfer*
bulb	die Birne	*dee beerner*
11 pedal	das Pedal	*dass pedarl*
12 pump	die Pumpe	*dee poomper*
13 reflector	der Rückstrahler	*dayr ruekshtrarler*
14 break pad	die Bremsbacke	*dee bremzbakker*
15 brake cable	das Bremskabel	*dass bremzkarbel*
16 ring lock	das Sicherheitsschloss	*dass zikherhaitsshloss*
17 carrier straps	das Spannband	*dass shpannbant*
tachometer	der Tacho(meter)	*dayr takhomayter*
18 spoke	die Speiche	*die shpaikher*
19 mudguard	das Schutzblech	*dass shootsblekh*
20 handlebar	der Lenker	*dayr lenker*
21 chain wheel	das Zahnrad	*dass tsarnrart*
toe clip	der Rennhaken	*dayr renharken*
22 crank axle	die Tretwelle	*dee traytveller*
drum brake	die Trommelbremse	*dee trommelbremzer*
rim	die Felge	*dee felger*
23 valve	das Ventil	*dass venteel*
24 valve tube	der Ventilschlauch	*dayr venteelshlowkh*
25 gear cable	das Gangschaltungskabel	*dass gangshaltoongskarbel*
26 fork	die Vorderradgabel	*dee forderrartgarbel*
27 front wheel	das Vorderrad	*dass forderrart*
28 seat	der Sattel	*dayr zattel*

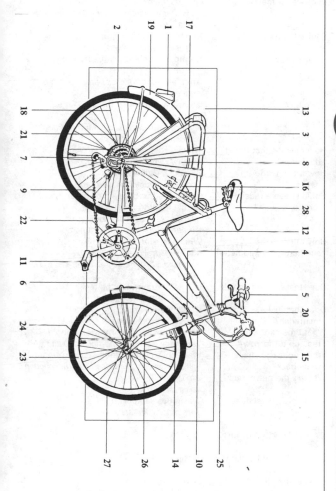

5 .9 **R**enting a vehicle

I'd like to rent a... _____	Ich möchte ein(en)...mieten
	ikh moekhter ain(en)...meeten
Do I need a (special) _____ licence for that?	Brauche ich dafür einen (bestimmten) Führerschein?
	browkher ikh dafuer ainen (beshtimmten) fuehrershain?
I'd like to rent the...for... ___	Ich möchte den/das...für...mieten
	ikh moekhter dayn/dass...fuer...meeten
– one day _____	Ich möchte den/das...für einen Tag mieten
	ikh moekhter dayn/dass...fuer ainen tark meeten
– two days _____	Ich möchte den/da ...für zwei Tage mieten
	ikh moekhter dayn/dass...fuer tsvai targer meeten
How much is that per_____ day/week?	Wieviel kostet das pro Tag/Woche?
	veefeel kostet dass pro tark/vokher?
How much is the _____ deposit?	Wie hoch ist die Kaution?
	vee hokh ist dee kowtseeoan?
Could I have a receipt _____ for the deposit?	Geben Sie mir bitte eine Quittung, dass ich die Kaution bezahlt habe
	gayben zee meer bitter ainer kvittoong, dass ikh dee kowtseeoan betsarlt harber
How much is the _____ surcharge per kilometre?	Wie hoch ist der zusätzliche Kilometerpreis?
	vee hokh ist dayr tsoo zetslikher kilo mayter praiss?
Does that include petrol? __	Ist das Benzin mit enthalten?
	ist dass bentseen mit enthalten?
Does that include _____ insurance?	Ist die Versicherung mit enthalten?
	ist dee fairsikhe roong mit enthalten?
What time can I pick_____ the...up tomorrow?	Wann kann ich das...morgen abholen?
	vann kann ikh dass...morgen apholen?
When does the...have _____ to be back?	Wann muss ich den/das...zurückbringen?
	vann mooss ikh dayn/dass...tsooruekbringen?
Where's the petrol tank? ___	Wo ist der Tank?
	vo ist dayr tank?
What sort of fuel does _____ it take?	Was muss ich tanken?
	vass mooss ikh tanken?

5 .10 **H**itchhiking

Where are you heading? ___	Wohin fahren Sie?
	vohin fahren zee?
Can I come along? _____	Darf ich mit Ihnen mitfahren?
	darf ikh mit eenen mit fahren?
Can my boyfriend/ _____ girlfriend come too?	Darf mein Freund/meine Freundin auch mit?
	darf main froynt/mainer froyndin owkh mitt?
I'm trying to get to... _____	Ich muss nach ...
	ikh mooss nakh ...
Is that on the way to...? _____	Liegt das auf dem Weg nach...
	leekt dass owf daym vayk nakh...

Could you drop me off...?	Könnten Sie mich absetzen?
	koennten zee mikh apsetsen?
– here?	Könnten Sie mich hier absetzen?
	koennten zee mikh heer apsetsen?
– at the...exit?	Könnten Sie mich an der Ausfahrt nach... absetzen?
	koennten zee mikh an dayr owsfahrt nakh... apsetsen?
– in the centre?	Könnten Sie mich im Zentrum absetzen?
	koennten zee mikh im tsentroom apsetsen?
– at the next roundabout?	Könnten Sie mich beim nächsten Kreisel/Kreisverkehr absetzen?
	koennten zee mikh baim nexten kraizel/krais fair kayr apzetsen?
Could you stop here, please?	Würden Sie bitte hier halten?
	vuerden zee bitter heer halten?
I'd like to get out here	Ich möchte hier raus
	ikh moekhter heer rows
Thanks for the lift	Vielen Dank fürs Mitnehmen
	feelen dunk fuers mitnaymen

Public transport

Public transport

.1 In general

● **Public transport** in Germany prides itself for being on time. Strikes (*Streiks*) are rare and only tend to occur around the trade unions' negotiations on pay which take place once a year. Tickets for buses can be bought as you get on the bus. Some unlimited travel cards/runabout tickets purchased for use on trains also cover all public means of transport within a designated area (*Verkehrsverbund*). Train tickets can be purchased either at the ticket office in the station or at ticket machines on the platforms.

Announcements

Der Zug nach...von...hat _____ eine Verspätung von...Minuten	The train to...from has been delayed by...minutes.
Auf Gleis ... fährt ein der Zug _____ nach.../aus...	The train now arriving at platform...is the train to.../from...
Auf Gleis...steht der Zug zur Abfahrt ____ bereit nach...	The train to...is about to leave from platform...
Achtung! Bitte zurückbleiben! _____ Ein Intercity fährt durch auf Gleis...	Attention please, keep your distance from the rail track, an intercity train will pass on platform...
Wir nähern uns (der Station/dem _____ Hauptbahnhof)...	We're now approaching...(the station/ main station)

Where does this train_____ go to?	Wohin fährt dieser Zug?	*vohinn fairt deezer tsook?*
Does this boat go to...? ____	Fährt dieses Schiff nach ...?	*fairt deezes shiff nakh...?*
Can I take this bus to...? ___	Kann ich mit diesem Bus nach...fahren?	*kann ikh mitt deezem boos nakh...fahren?*
Does this train stop at...? _	Hält dieser Zug in...?	*helt deezer tsook in...?*
Is this seat taken/free/ _____ reserved?	Ist dieser Platz besetzt/frei/reserviert?	*ist deezer plats bezetst/frai/rezerveert?*
I've booked... _____	Ich habe ... reservieren lassen	*ikh haber ... rezerveeren lassen*
Could you tell me _____ where I have to get off for... ?	Könnten Sie mir sagen, wo ich aussteigen muss, um zu/zum/zur/zu den ... zu kommen?	*koennten zee meer zargen, vo ikh ows shtaigen mooss, oom tsoo/tsoom/tsoor/tsoo dayn ... tsoo kommen?*
Could you let me_____ know when we get to...?	Würden Sie mir bitte Bescheid sagen, wenn wir bei/beim/bei der/bei den ... sind?	*vuerden zee meer bitter beshait zargen, venn veer bai/baim/bai dayr/bai dayn ... zint?*

Could you stop at the next stop, please?	Halten Sie bitte an der nächsten Haltestelle
	halten zee bitter an dayr nexten halter shteller
Where are we now?	Wo sind wir hier?
	vo zint veer heer?
Do I have to get off here?	Muss ich hier aussteigen?
	mooss ikh heer ows shtaigen?
Have we already passed...?	Sind wir schon an/am/an der ... vorbei?
	zint veer shoan an/am/an dayr ... forbai?
How long have I been asleep?	Wie lange habe ich geschlafen?
	vee langer harber ikh geshlarfen?
How long does... stop here?	Wie lange bleibt der/die ... heer stehen?
	vee langer blaipt dayr/dee ... heer shtayhen?
Can I come back on the same ticket?	Kann ich mit dieser Fahrkarte auch wieder zurück?
	kann ikh mit deezer farkarter owkh veeder tsooruek?
Can I change on this ticket?	Kann ich mit dieser Fahrkarte umsteigen?
	kann ikh mit deezer farkarter oom shtaigen?
How long is this ticket valid for?	Wie lange ist diese Fahrkarte gültig?
	vee langer ist deezer farkarter gueltikh?
How much is the supplement for the intercity?	Wie hoch ist der IC Zuschlag?
	vee hokh ist der ee tsee tsooschlark?

6 .2 Questions to passengers

Ticket types

Erster oder zweiter Klasse?	First or second class?
Einfach oder hin und zurück/Hin- und Rückfahrt?	Single or return?
Raucher oder Nichtraucher?	Smoking or non-smoking?
Am Fenster oder am Gang?	Window or aisle?
Vorn oder hinten?	Front or back?
Sitzplatz oder Liegewagen?	Seat or couchette?
Oben, in der Mitte oder unten?	Top, middle or bottom?
Touristenklasse oder Business Class?	Tourist class or business class?
Kabine oder Sitzplatz?	Cabin or seat?
Einzel- oder Doppelkabine?	Single or double?
Zu wieviel Personen reisen Sie?	How many are travelling?

Destination

Wohin reisen Sie? _____	Where are you travelling?
Wann reisen Sie ab? _____	When are you leaving?
Abfahrt/(aircraft) Abflug um..._____	Your...leaves at...
Sie müssen in...umsteigen_____	You have to change trains at...
Sie müssen in...aussteigen _____	You have to get off at...
Sie müssen über...reisen _____	You have to travel via...
Die Hinreise fängt am...an _____	The outward journey is on...
Die Rückreise beginnt am...	The return journey is on...
Sie müssen spätestens...an Bord sein ___	You have to be on board by...

Inside the vehicle

Ihre Fahrkarte bitte_____	Your ticket, please
Ihre Reservierung bitte _____	Your reservation, please
Ihren (Reise)pass bitte_____	Your passport, please
Sie sitzen auf dem falschen Platz_____	You're in the wrong seat
Sie sitzen im/in der falschen... _____	You're on/in the wrong...
Dieser Platz ist reserviert _____	This seat is reserved
Sie müssen einen Zuschlag (be)zahlen ___	You'll have to pay a supplement
Der/die/das...hat eine Verspätung von ___ ...Minuten	The...has been delayed by...minutes

6 .3 Tickets

Where can I...? _____	Wo kann ich...?
	vo kann ikh...?
– buy a ticket?_____	Wo kann ich eine Karte kaufen?
	vo kann ikh ainer karter kowfen?
– make a reservation? _____	Wo kann ich einen Platz reservieren lassen?
	vo kann ikh ainen plats rezerveeren lassen?
– book a flight?_____	Wo kann ich einen Flug buchen?
	vo kann ikh ainen flook bookhen?
Could I have a...to..., please? _____	Ich möchte...nach...
	ikh moekhter...nakh...
– a single _____	Ich möchte einmal einfach nach...
	ikh moekhter ainmarl ainfakh nakh...
– a return _____	Ich möchte eine Rückfahrkarte nach...
	ikh moekhter ainer ruekfarkarter nakh...
first class _____	erster Klasse
	airster klasser
second class _____	zweiter Klasse
	tsvaiter klasser
tourist class_____	Touristenklasse
	tooristen klasser

Public transport

6

business class _____	Business Class
	bizniss klarss
I'd like to book a _____ seat/couchette/cabin	Ich möchte einen Sitzplatz/Liegewagen-platz/eine Kabine reservieren lassen
	ikh moekhter ainen zits plats/leeger vargen plats/ainer kabiner rezerveeren
I'd like to book a berth in __ the sleeping car	Ich möchte einen Platz im Schlafwagen reservieren lassen
	ikh moekhter ainen plats im shlarfvargen rezerveeren lassen
top/middle/bottom _____	oben/in der Mitte/unten
	oaben/in dayr mitter/oonten
smoking/no smoking _____	Raucher/Nichtraucher
	rowkher/nikht rowkher
by the window _____	am Fenster
	am fenster
single/double _____	Einzel-/Doppel-
	aintsel-/doppel-
at the front/back_____	vorn/hinten
	forn/hinten
There are...of us_____	Wir sind zu ...t (e.g. zweit, dritt, viert)
	veer zint tsoo ...t (e.g. tsvait, dritt, feert)
a car _____	ein Auto
	ain owto
a caravan _____	ein Wohnwagen
	ain voanvargen
...bicycles_____	...Fahrräder
	...fahr rayder
Do you also have...? _____	Haben Sie...?
	harben zee...?
– season tickets? _____	Haben Sie Sammelfahrscheine?
	harben zee zammel fahr shainer?
– weekly tickets? _____	Haben Sie Wochenkarten?
	harben zee vokhen karten?
– monthly season tickets?__	Haben Sie Monatskarten?
	harben zee moanarts karten?
Where's? _____	Wo ist...?

6.4 Information

	vo ist...?
Where's the information ___ desk?	Wo ist die Auskunft?
	vo ist dee owskoonft?
Where can I find a_____ timetable?	Wo ist die Tafel mit den Abfahrtszeiten/Ankunftszeiten?
	vo ist dee tarfel mit den apfahrtstsaiten/ankunftstsaiten?
Where's the...desk?_____	Wo ist der Schalter für...?
	vo ist dayr shalter fuer...?
Do you have a city map____ with the bus/the underground routes on it?	Haben Sie einen Stadtplan mit dem Bus-/U-Bahnnetz?
	harben zee ainen shtatplarn mit dem booss-/oobarn nets?
Do you have a _____ timetable?	Haben Sie einen Fahrplan?
	harben zee ainen farplarn?

I'd like to confirm/ cancel/change my booking for/trip to...	Ich möchte meine Reservierung/Reise nach...bestätigen/annullieren/ändern *ikh moekhter mainer rezerveerung/raizer nakh ... beshtaytigen/annoo leeren/endern*
Will I get my money back?	Bekomme ich mein Geld zurück? *bekommer ikh main gelt tsooruek?*
I want to go to... How do I get there? (What's the quickest way there?)	Ich muss nach... Wie komme ich da (am schnellsten) hin? *ikh mooss nakh... vee kommer ikh da (am shnellsten) hin?*
How much is a single/return to...?	Wieviel kostet eine Fahrt/Rückfahrkarte nach...? *veefeel kostet ainer fart/ruek fahr karter nakh...?*
Do I have to pay a supplement?	Muss ich Zuschlag zahlen? *mooss ikh tsooshlak tsarlen?*
Can I interrupt my journey with this ticket?	Darf ich die Reise mit diesem Ticket unterbrechen? *darf ikh dee raizer mit deezem ticket oonter brekhen?*
How much luggage am I allowed?	Wieviel Gepäck darf ich mitnehmen? *veefeel gepeck darf ikh mitnaymen?*
Does this...travel direct?	Geht diese(r)/dieses ... direkt? *gayt deeze(r)/deezes ... direkt?*
Do I have to change? Where?	Muss ich umsteigen? Wo? *mooss ikh oom shtaigen? vo?*
Will there be any stopovers?	Macht das Flugzeug eine Zwischenlandung? *makht dass flooktsoyk ainer tsvishen landoong?*
Does the boat call in at any ports on the way?	Legt das Schiff unterwegs in irgendwelchen Häfen an? *laykt dass shiff oontervegz in eergent velkhen hayfen an?*
Does the train/ bus stop at...?	Hält der Zug/Bus in...? *helt der tsook/booss in...?*
Where should I get off?	Wo muss ich aussteigen? *vo mooss ikh ows shtaigen?*
Is there a connection to...?	Gibt es einen Anschluss nach...? *gipt ez ainen anschluss nakh...?*
How long do I have to wait?	Wie lange muss ich warten? *vee langer mooss ikh varten?*
When does...leave?	Wann fährt...ab? *vann fairt...ap?*
What time does the first/next/last...leave?	Wann fährt/(aircraft) fliegt der/die/das erste/nächste/letzte...? *vann fairt/fleekt dayr/dee/dass airster/nexter/letster...?*
How long does...take?	Wie lange dauert die Fahrt/(flight) der Flug? *vee langer dowert dee fahrt/dayr flook?*
What time does...arrive in...?	Wann kommt...in...an? *vann kommt...in...an?*
Where does the...to... leave from?	Wo fährt/(aircraft) fliegt der/die/das nach ...ab? *vo fairt/fleekt dayr/dee/duss nakh...ap?*
Is this...to...?	Ist dies ... nach...? *ist deez ... nakh...?*

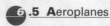 .5 **A**eroplanes

● **On arrival** at a German airport (Flughafen), you will find the following signs:

Abflug Inland/Ausland	domestic/international departures	Ankunft arrivals

After the check-in a boarding pass (Bordkarte, Einsteigekarte) is handed out which details the gate (Flugsteig) and departure time (Abflugzeit).

.6 **T**rains

● **The rail network** is extensive. The Deutsche Bundesbahn is responsible for the national rail traffic. Generally there are four types of trains: *Intercity, Eilzug/Schnellzug* (fast train which does not stop at small stations - long distance), *S-Bahn* (designed to link smaller towns and villages on the outskirts with the city centre), *U-Bahn* (underground). A supplement is only to be paid for the *Intercity*. Seats can be reserved in advance on the *Intercity* and *Eilzug* only.

.7 **T**axis

● **In nearly all** large cities and bigger towns, there are plenty of taxis. Although German taxis have no fixed colour, they tend to be cream coloured. Virtually all taxis have a meter.

Besetzt booked	Frei for hire	Taxistand taxi rank

Taxi! _____	Taxi! *tarksi!*
Could you get me a taxi, ___ please?	Würden Sie mir bitte ein Taxi/eine Taxe bestellen? *vuerden zee meer bitter ain tarksi/ainer tarkser beshtellen?*
Where can I find a taxi_____ around here?	Wo finde ich hier in der Nähe ein Taxi? *vo finder ikh heer in dayr nayher ain tarksi?*
Could you take me to..., ___ please?	Zu/zum/zur ... bitte *tsoo/tsoom/tsoor ... bitter*
– this address _____	Zu dieser Adresse bitte *tsoo deezer adresser bitter*
– the...hotel _____	Zum Hotel ... bitte *tsoom hotel ... bitter*
– the town/city centre_____	Ins Zentrum bitte *ins tsentroom bitter*
– the station _____	Zum Bahnhof bitte *tsoom barnhoaf bitter*
– the airport _____	Zum Flughafen bitte *tsoom flook harfen bitter*
How much is the _____ trip to...?	Wieviel kostet die Fahrt zu/zum/zur...? *veefeel kostet dee fart tsoo/tsoom/tsoor...?*

How far is it to...?	Wie weit ist es nach ...?
	vee vait ist ez nakh ...?
Could you turn on the meter, please?	Würden Sie bitte das Taxameter einschalten?
	vuerden zee bitter dass taksarmeter ainshalten?
I'm in a hurry	Ich habe es eilig
	ikh haber ez ailikh
Could you speed up/slow down a little?	Könnten Sie etwas schneller/langsamer fahren?
	koennten zee etvass shneller/langzarmer fahren?
Could you take a different route?	Könnten Sie eine andere Strecke fahren?
	koennten zee ainer anderer shtrekker fahren?
I'd like to get out here, please.	Lassen Sie mich hier aussteigen
	lassen zee mikh heer owsshtaigen
You have to go...here	Sie müssen gehen...
	zee muessen gayhen...
You have to go straight on here.	hier geradeaus
	heer gerarder ows
You have to turn left here	hier (nach) links
	heer (nakh) links
You have to turn right here.	hier (nach) rechts
	heer (nakh) rekhts
This is it	Hier ist es
	heer ist ez
Could you wait a minute for me, please?	Warten Sie bitte einen Augenblick
	varten zee bitter ainen owgenblick

6

Public transport

Overnight accommodation

7 Overnight accommodation

7 .1 General

● **There is a great variety** in overnight accommodation in Germany.
Hotels: the 'star-system' does not tend to be operational in Germany.
However, some are hotels '*vom ADAC empfohlen*' (recommended by
the German motoring organisation) promising good standard. Most
hotels offer *Halbpension* (half board) or *Vollpension* (full board).
Pension/Gasthof/Gästehaus: often smaller houses with B + B type
accommodation. A *Gasthof* would also have a restaurant.
Rasthof: accommodation available at motorway service stations.
Ferienwohnungen: holiday flats available in many tourist places,
recreational centres and/or camping sites.
Berghütten: mountain hut providing basic sleeping space.
Jugendherberge: Youth Hostels in Germany require an international
Youth Hostel pass and usually expect clients to provide their own linen.
Campingplatz: free camping is not allowed in Germany. Camping sites
are usually privately run and not open all year round.

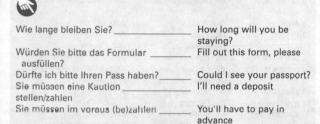

Wie lange bleiben Sie? _____	How long will you be staying?
Würden Sie bitte das Formular _____ ausfüllen?	Fill out this form, please
Dürfte ich bitte Ihren Pass haben?_____	Could I see your passport?
Sie müssen eine Kaution _____ stellen/zahlen	I'll need a deposit
Sie müssen im voraus (be)zahlen _____	You'll have to pay in advance

My name's...I've made_____ a reservation over the phone/by mail	Mein Name ist...Ich habe einen Platz reservieren lassen (telefonisch/schriftlich) *main narmer ist...ikh harber ainen plats rezerveeren lassen (telefoanish/shriftlikh)*
How much is it per _____ night/week/ month?	Wieviel kostet es pro Nacht/Woche/Monat? *veefeel kostet ez pro nakht/vokher/moanart?*
We'll be staying at _____ least...nights/weeks	Wir bleiben mindestens...Nächte/Wochen *veer blaiben mindestens...nekhter/vokhen*
We don't know yet _____	Das wissen wir noch nicht genau *dass vissen veer nokh nikht genow*
Do you allow pets _____ (cats/dogs)?	Sind Haustiere (Hunde/Katzen) erlaubt? *zint howzteerer (hunder/katsen) erlowpt?*
What time does the _____ gate/door open/close?	Wann ist die Pforte/Tür geöffnet/(auf)/geschlossen/(zu)? *van ist dee pforter/tuer geoeffnet/(owf)/geschlossen/(tsoo)?*
Could you get me _____ a taxi, please?	Würden Sie mir bitte ein Taxi bestellen? *vuerden zee meer bitter ain tarksi beshtellen?*
Is there any mail _____ for me?	Ist Post für mich da? *ist posst fuer mikh dar?*

Overnight accommodation

7

Camping equipment
(the diagram shows the numbered parts)

	luggage space	das Gepäckapsis	*dass gepekapsis*
	can opener	der Dosenöffner	*dayr doazenoefner*
	butane gas bottle	die Butangasflasche	*dee bootarn gasflasher*
1	pannier	die Packtasche	*dee pakktasher*
2	gas cooker	der Gaskocher	*dayr gasskokher*
3	groundsheet	die Bodenplane	*dee boadenplarner*
	mallet	der Hammer	*dayr hammer*
	hammock	die Hängematte	*dee hengermatter*
4	jerry can	der Kanister	*dayr kannister*
	campfire	das Lagerfeuer	*dass largerfoyer*
5	folding chair	der Klappstuhl	*dayr klapshtool*
6	insulated picnic box	die Kühltasche	*dee kuehltasher*
	ice pack	das Kühlelement	*dass kuehlelement*
	compass	der Kompass	*dayr kompas*
	wick	der Glühstrumpf	*dayr gluehshtroompf*
	corkscrew	der Korkenzieher	*dayr korkentseeyer*
7	airbed	die Luftmatratze	*dee looftmatrattser*
8	airbed plug pump	der Matratzenstöpsel	*dayr matrattsenshtoepsel*
9	awning	das Vordach	*dass fordakh*
10	karimat	die Matte	*dee matter*
11	pan	die Pfanne	*dee pfanner*
12	pan handle	der Pfannenstiel	*dayr pfannenshteel*
	primus stove	der Petroleumkocher	*dayr petroaleyoomkokher*
	zip	der Reissverschluss	*dayr raissfershluss*
13	backpack	der Rucksack	*dayr rookzakk*
14	guy rope	die Zeltleine	*dee tseltlainer*
	sleeping bag	der Schlafsack	*dayr shlarfzak*
15	storm lantern	die Sturmlaterne	*dee shtoormlaterner*
	camp bed	die Liege	*leeger*
	table	der Tisch	*dayr tish*
16	tent	das Zelt	*dass tselt*
17	tent peg	der Hering	*dayr hayring*
18	tent pole	die Zeltstange	*dee tseltshtanger*
	vacuum flask	die Thermosflasche	*dee termowsflasher*
19	water bottle	die Feldflasche	*dee feltflasher*
	clothes peg	die Wäscheklammer	*dee vesherklummer*
	clothes line	die Wäscheleine	*dee vesherlainer*
	windbreak	der Windschutz	*dayr vintshoots*
20	torch	die Taschenlampe	*dee tashenlamper*
	pocket knife	das Taschenmesser	*dass tashenmesser*

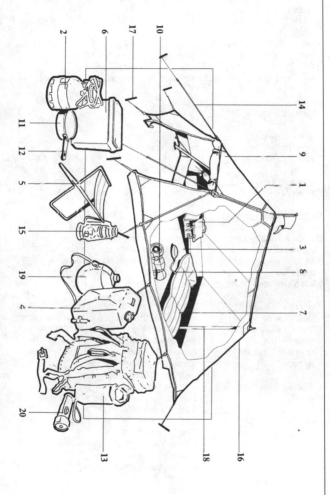

7 .2 Camping

See the diagram on page 69.

Sie können sich selbst einen Platz aussuchen	You can pick your own site
Sie bekommen einen Platz zugewiesen	You'll be allocated a site
Dies ist Ihre Platznummer	This is your site number.
Kleben Sie dies bitte auf Ihr Auto	Stick this on your car, please.
Sie dürfen diese Karte nicht verlieren	Please don't lose this card

Where's the manager?	Wo ist der Verwalter?
	vo ist der fairvalter?
Are we allowed to camp here?	Dürfen wir hier campen?
	duerfen veer heer kampen?
There are...of us and ...tents	Wir sind ... Personen und haben ... Zelte
	veer zint ... perzoanen oont harben ... tselter
Can we pick our own site?	Dürfen wir selbst einen Platz aussuchen?
	duerfen veer zelpst ainen plats ows zookhen?
Do you have a quiet spot for us?	Haben Sie einen ruhigen Platz für uns?
	harben zee ainen roohigen plats fuer oons?
Do you have any other sites available?	Haben Sie keinen anderen freien Platz?
	harben zee kainen anderen fraien plats?
It's too windy/sunny/ shady here.	Hier ist zuviel Wind/Sonne/Schatten
	heer ist tsoofeel vint/zonner/shatten
It's too crowded here	Hier ist es zu voll
	heer ist es tsoo foll
The ground's too hard/uneven	Der Boden ist zu hart/ungleichmässig
	der boaden ist tsoo hart/oon glaikh mayssikh
Do you have a level spot for the camper/caravan/folding caravan?	Haben Sie einen horizontalen Platz für das Wohnmobil/den Wohnwagen/Faltwagen?
	harben zee ainen horitsontarlen plats fuer dass voan moabeel/dayn voanvargen/faltvargen?
Could we have adjoining sites?	Können wir beieinander stehen?
	koennen veer baiainander shtayhen?
Can we park the car next to the tent?	Darf das Auto beim Zelt geparkt werden?
	darf dass owto baim tselt geparkt verden?
How much is it per person/tent/caravan/car?	Was kostet es pro Person/Zelt/Wohnwagen/Auto?
	vass kostet ez pro perzoan/tselt/voanvargen/owto?
Are there any...?	Gibt es...?
	gipt ez...?
– any hot showers?	Warmwasserduschen?
	varm vasser dooshen?
– washing machines?	Waschmaschinen?
	wash masheenen?
Is there a...on the site?	Gibt es auf dem Gelände...?
	gipt ez owf daym gelender...?

Overnight accommodation | **7**

70

Is there a children's_____ play area on the site?	...einen Kinderspielplatz? *...ainen kinder shpeel plats?*
Are there covered _____ cooking facilities on the site?	...eine überdachte Kochgelegenheit? *...ainer ueber dakhter kokh gelaygen hait?*
Can I rent a safe here?_____	Kann ich hier ein Schliessfach mieten? *kann ikh heer ain shleesfakh meeten?*
Are we allowed to_____ barbecue here?	Darf man hier grillen? *darf man heer grillen?*
Are there any power_____ points?	Gibt es Elektroanschlüsse? *gipt ez elektro anshluesser?*
When's the rubbish_____ collected?	Wann wird der Abfall abgeholt? *vann virt dayr apfal apgeholt?*
Do you sell gas bottles ____ (butane gas/propane gas)?	Verkaufen Sie Gasflaschen (Butangas/Propangas)? *fairkowfen zee gassflashen (bootarn gass/proparn gass)?*

🦻.3 Hotel/B&B/apartment/holiday house

Do you have a _____ single/double room available?	Haben Sie ein Einzelzimmer/Doppelzimmer frei? *harben zee ain aintsel tsimmer/doppel tsimmer frai?*
per person/per room _ __	pro Person/pro Zimmer *pro perzoan/pro tsimmer*
Does that include __ _____ breakfast/lunch/dinner?	Ist das einschliesslich Frühstück/Mittagessen/Abendessen? *ist dass ainshleeslikh frueh shtuek/mittark essen/arbent essen?*
Could we have two_____ adjoining rooms?	Können wir zwei Zimmer nebeneinander bekommen? *koennen veer tsvai tsimmer nayben ainander bekommen?*
with/without ___ _ __ toilet/bath/shower	Mit/ohne eigener Toilette/eigenem Bad/eigener Dusche *mit/oaner aigener twaletter/aigenem bart/aigener doosher*
(not) facing the street_____	(nicht) an der Strassenseite *(nikht) an dayr shtrassen zaiter*
with/without a view _____ of the sea	mit/ohne Seesicht *mit/oaner zayzikht*
Is there...in the hotel?_____	Gibt es im Hotel...? *gipt ez im hotel...?*
Is there a lift in the _____ hotel?	Gibt es im Hotel einen Fahrstuhl? *gipt ez im hotel ainen fahrshtool?*
Do you have room _____ service?	Gibt es im Hotel Zimmerservice? *gipt ez im hotel tsimmer zairviss?*
Could I see the room? ____	Könnte ich das Zimmer mal sehen? *koennter ikh dass tsimmer marl zayhen?*
I'll take this room_____	Ich nehme dieses Zimmer *ikh naymer deezes tsimmer*
We don't like this one ____	Dieses gefällt uns nicht *deezes gefellt oons nikht*

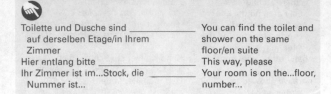

Toilette und Dusche sind _____ auf derselben Etage/in Ihrem Zimmer	You can find the toilet and shower on the same floor/en suite
Hier entlang bitte _____	This way, please
Ihr Zimmer ist im...Stock, die _____ Nummer ist...	Your room is on the...floor, number...

Do you have a larger/_____ less expensive room?	Haben Sie ein grösseres/billigeres Zimmer?
	harben zee ain groesseres/billeegeres tsimmer?
Could you put in a cot? ___	Können Sie ein Kinderbett dazustellen?
	koennen zee ain kinder bet datsoo shtellen?
What time's breakfast? ___	Ab wann gibt es Frühstück?
	ap vann gipt ez frueh shtuek?
Where's the dining _____ room?	Wo ist der Speisesaal?
	vo ist dayr shpaize zarl?
Can I have breakfast _____ in my room?	Kann ich Frühstück aufs Zimmer bekommen?
	kann ikh frueh shtuek owfs tsimmer bekommen?
Where's the emergency _____ exit/fire escape?	Wo ist der Notausgang/die Feuertreppe?
	vo ist der noat owsgang/dee foyer trepper?
Where can I park my _____ car (safely)?	Wo kann ich mein Auto (sicher) abstellen?
	vo kann ikh main owto (zikher) apshtellen?
The key to room..., _____ please	Den Schlüssel für Zimmer...bitte
	dayn shluessel fuer tsimmer...bitter
Could you put this in _____ the safe, please?	Darf ich dies bitte in Ihren Safe legen?
	darf ikh dees bitter in eeren safe laygen?
Could you wake me _____ at...tomorrow?	Wecken Sie mich morgen bitte um...Uhr
	vekken zee mikh morgen bitter oom...ooer
Could you find a _____ babysitter for me?	Können Sie mir einen Babysitter besorgen?
	koennen zee meer ainen babysitter bezorgen?
Could I have an extra _____ blanket?	Würden Sie bitte eine extra Decke bringen?
	vuerden zee bitter ainer ekstrar dekker bringen?
What days do the _____ cleaners come in?	An welchen Tagen wird saubergemacht?
	an velkhen targen virt zowber gemakht?
When are the sheets/ _____ towels/tea towels changed?	Wann werden die Bettlaken/Handtücher/Geschirrtücher gewechselt?
	vann verden dee bett larken/hant tuekher/geshirr tuekher gevekhselt?

7

Overnight accommodation

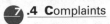

7 .4 Complaints

We can't sleep for _____ the noise	Wir können durch den Lärm nicht schlafen *veer koennen doorkh den lerm nikht shlarfen*
Could you turn the _____ radio down, please?	Könnten Sie das Radio bitte etwas leiser stellen? *koennten zee dass radeeo bitter etvass laizer shtellen?*
We're out of toilet paper ___	Das Toilettenpapier ist alle *dass twaletten papeer ist aller*
There aren't any.../ _____ there's not enough...	Es gibt keine.../nicht genug... *es gipt kainer.../nikht genook ...*
The bed linen's dirty_____	Die Bettwäsche ist schmutzig *dee bettvesher ist shmootsikh*
The room hasn't been _____ cleaned.	Das Zimmer ist nicht saubergemacht *dass tsimmer ist nikht zowber gemakht*
The kitchen is not clean___	Die Küche ist nicht sauber *dee kuekher ist nikht zowber*
The kitchen utensils are___ dirty	Die Küchengeräte sind schmutzig *dee kuekhen gerayter zint shmootsikh*
The heater's not_____ working	Die Heizung funktioniert nicht *dee haitsoong foonk tseeoneert nikht*
There's no (hot) _____ water/electricity	Es gibt kein (warmes) Wasser/keinen Strom *ez gipt kain (varmez) vasser/kainen shtroam*
...is broken_____	... ist kaputt *... ist kapoott*
Could you have that_____ seen to?	Können Sie das in Ordnung bringen lassen? *koennen zee dass in ordnoong bringen lassen?*
Could I have another _____ room/site?	Könnte ich ein anderes Zimmer/einen anderen Stellplatz bekommen? *koennter ikh ain underes tsimmer/ainen anderen stellplats bekommen?*
The bed creaks terribly	Das Bett knarrt furchtbar *dass bet knarrt foorkhtbar*
The bed sags _____	Das Bett biegt sich durch *dass bet beekt zikh doorkh*
Could we have a _____ board to put underneath?	Haben Sie ein Brett zum Drunterlegen? *harben zee ain bret tsôom droonter laygen?*
It's too noisy _____	Es ist zu laut *ez ist tsoo lowt*
We have trouble _____ with bugs/ insects	Wir haben Ärger mit Ungeziefer/Insekten *veer harben airger mit oongetseefer/ inzekten*
This place is full_____ of mosquitoes	Es wimmelt hier von Mücken *ez vimmelt heer fon mueken*
– cockroaches_____	Es wimmelt hier von Kakerlaken *ez vimmelt heer fon karker larken*

7 Overnight accommodation

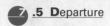

7.5 Departure

See also 8.2 Settling the bill

I'm leaving tomorrow. Could I settle my bill, please?	Ich reise morgen ab. Könnte ich jetzt bitte abrechnen?
	ikh raizer morgen ap. koennter ikh yetst bitter aprekhnen?
What time should we vacate?	Wann müssen wir den/das/die... verlassen?
	vann muessen veer dayn/dass/dee... fairlassen?
Could I have my deposit/ passport back, please?	Würden Sie mir bitte die Kaution/den Pass wiedergeben?
	vuerden zee meer bitter dee kowtseeoan/dayn pass veeder gayben?
We're in a terrible hurry	Wir haben grosse Eile
	veer harben groasser ailer
Could you forward my mail to this address?	Würden Sie mir bitte die Post an diese Adresse nachschicken?
	vuerden zee meer bitter dee posst an deezer adresser nakh shikken?
Could we leave our luggage here until we leave?	Dürfen wir unsere Koffer bis zur Abreise hier stehenlassen?
	duerfen veer oonzere koffer biss tsoor apraizer heer shtayen lassen?
Thanks for your hospitality	Vielen Dank für die Gastlichkeit/die Gastfreundschaft
	feelen dunk fuer dee gastlikh kait/dee gast froynt shaft

7

Overnight accommodation

Money matters

Money matters

● **In general**, banks are open to the public between 9 am and 4.30 pm. Some types of bank, smaller outlets and banks in smaller towns and villages often close for lunch between 12 noon and 2 pm. Banks are closed on a Saturday. To exchange currency a proof of identity is usually required. The sign Geld/wechsel/ausländische Währung indicates that money can be changed. Hotels may also offer exchange facilities but at less favourable rates.

8 .1 **B**anks

Where can I find a _____ bank/an exchange office around here?

Wo ist hier eine Bank/eine Wechselstube?
vo ist heer ainer bank/ainer vekhsel shtoober?

Where can I cash this_____ traveller's cheque/giro cheque?

Wo kann ich diesen Reisescheck/Postbarscheck einlösen?
vo kann ikh deezen raizer shekk/postbar shekk ainloezen?

Can I cash this...here? _____

Kann ich hier diesen ... einlösen?
kann ikh heer deezen ... ainloezen?

Can I withdraw money_____ on my credit card here?

Kann ich hier mit einer Kreditkarte Geld bekommen?
kann ikh heer mit ainer kredit karter gelt bekommen?

What's the minimum/_____ maximum amount?

Was ist das Minimum/Maximum?
vass ist dass minimoom/maksimoom?

Can I take out less_____ than that?

Darf ich auch weniger abheben?
darf ikh owkh vayniger aphayben?

I've had some money_____ transferred here. Has it arrived yet?

Ich habe Geld überweisen lassen. Ist es schon eingegangen?
ikh harber gelt ueber vaizen lassen. ist ez shoan ain gegangen?

These are the details _____ of my bank in the UK

Dies sind die Angaben von meiner Bank in England
deez zint dee angarben fon mainer bank in englant

This is my bank/giro_____ number

Dies ist meine Kontonummer/ Gironummer
deez ist mainer konto noomer/geero noomer

I'd like to change _____ some money
– pounds into... _____

Ich möchte Geld wechseln
ikh moekhter gelt vekhseln
– (englische) Pfund in...
– (englisher) pfoont in...

– dollars into... _____

– Dollars in...
– (dollars) in...

What's the exchange _____ rate?

Wie hoch ist der Wechselkurs?
vee hokh ist dayr vekhsel koors?

Could you give me _____ some small change with it?

Können Sie mir auch etwas Kleingeld geben?
koennen zee meer owkh etvass klaingelt gayben?

This is not right _____

Das stimmt nicht
dass shtimmt nikht

Money matters

8

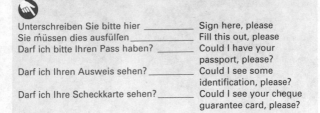

Unterschreiben Sie bitte hier _____	Sign here, please
Sie müssen dies ausfüllen _____	Fill this out, please
Darf ich bitte Ihren Pass haben? _____	Could I have your passport, please?
Darf ich Ihren Ausweis sehen? _____	Could I see some identification, please?
Darf ich Ihre Scheckkarte sehen? _____	Could I see your cheque guarantee card, please?

.2 Settling the bill

Could you put it on _____ my bill?	Könnten Sie das auf die Rechnung setzen?
	koennten zee dass owf dee rekhnoong setsen?
Does this amount _____ include service?	Ist die Bedienung in diesem Betrag enthalten?
	ist dee bedeenoong in deezem betrark enthalten?
Can I pay by...? _____	Kann ich mit...bezahlen?
	kann ikh mit...betsarlen?
Can I pay by credit card? ___	Kann ich mit (einer) Kreditkarte bezahlen?
	kann ikh mit (ainer) kredit karter betsarlen?
Can I pay by traveller's _____ cheque?	Kann ich mit einem Reisescheck bezahlen?
	kann ikh mit ainem raizer shekk betsarlen?
Can I pay with foreign _____ currency?	Kann ich in ausländischer Währung bezahlen?
	kann ikh in owslendisher vayroong betsarlen?
You've given me too _____ much/you haven't given me enough change	Sie haben mir zuviel/zuwenig (wieder)gegeben
	zee harben meer tsoofeel/tsoovaynikh (veeder) gegayben
Could you check this _____ again, please?	Würden Sie das noch mal nachrechnen?
	vuerden zee dass nokh marl nakh rekhnen?
Could I have a receipt, _____ please?	Ich hätte gern eine Quittung/den Kassenzettel
	ikh hetter gayrn ainer kvittoong/dayn kassen tsettel
I don't have enough _____ money on me	Ich habe nicht genug Geld bei mir
	ikh harber nikht genook gelt bai meer

Wir nehmen keine _____ Kreditkarten/Reiseschecks/Auslands währungen an	We don't accept credit cards/traveller's cheques/foreign currency

This is for you _____	Bitte, das ist für Sie
	bitter, dass ist fuer zee
Keep the change _____	Behalten Sie das Wechselgeld
	beharlten zee dass vekhselgelt

Post and telephone

9 Post and telephone

9.1 Post

For giros, see 8 Money matters

● **Post offices** are open from Monday to Friday between 8.30 am and 5 pm. In smaller towns the post office closes at lunch. On Saturdays they are open until 12 noon. Stamps are only available at post offices and some hotel receptions. Post boxes are yellow.

Briefmarken	Postanweisung	Telegramme
stamps	money orders	telegrams
Päckchen/Pakete		
parcels		

Where's...?	Wo ist...?
	vo ist...?
Where's the post office?	Wo ist hier ein Postamt?
	vo ist heer ain postamt?
Where's the main post office?	Wo ist die Hauptpost?
	vo ist dee howptpost?
Where's the postbox?	Wo ist hier ein Briefkasten?
	vo ist heer ain breefkasten?
Which counter should I go to...?	An welchem Schalter kann ich...?
	an velkhem shalter kann ikh...?
– to send a fax	An welchem Schalter kann ich telefaxen?
	an velkhem shalter kann ikh telefaksen?
– to change money	An welchem Schalter kann ich Geld wechseln?
	an velkhem shalter kann ikh gelt vekhseln?
– to change giro cheques	An welchem Schalter kann ich Schecks einlösen?
	an velkhem shalter kann ikh shekks ain loezen?
– for a Telegraph Money Order?	An welchem Schalter kann ich telegrafisch Geld überweisen?
	an velkhem shalter kann ikh telegrarfish gelt ueber vaizen?
Poste restante	Postlagernd
	postlargernt
Is there any mail for me. My name's...	Ist Post für mich da? Mein Name ist...
	ist post fuer mikh dar? main narmer ist...

Stamps

What's the postage for a...to...?	Wieviel muss auf einen/ein(e)...nach...?
	veefeel mooss owf ainen/ain(er)...nakh...?
Are there enough stamps on it?	Sind genug Briefmarken drauf?
	zint genook breefmarken drowf?
I'd like... ...mark stamps	Ich möchte...Briefmarken zu...
	ikh moekhter...breefmarken tsoo...
I'd like to send this...	Ich möchte dies...schicken
	ikh moekhter dees...shikken

– express _____	Ich möchte dies per Eilboten schicken *ikh moekhter dees payr ailboaten shikken*
– by air mail _____	Ich möchte dies per Luftpost schicken *ikh moekhter dees payr looftpost shikken*
– by registered mail _____	Ich möchte dies per Einschreiben schicken *ikh moekhter dees payr ainshraiben shikken*

Telegram/fax

I'd like to send a _____ telegram to...	Ich möchte ein Telegramm nach... aufgeben *ikh moekhter ain telegram nakh...* *owfgayben*
How much is that _____ per word?	Wieviel kostet das pro Wort? *veefeel kostet dass pro vort?*
This is the text I want_____ to send	Dies ist der Text des Telegramms *dees ist dayr tekst dess telegrams*
Shall I fill out the form_____ myself?	Soll ich das Formular selbst ausfüllen? *zoll ikh dass formoolar zelpst owsfuellen?*
Can I make photocopies/___ send a fax here?	Kann ich hier fotokopieren/telefaxen? *kann ikh heer foto kopeeren/telefaksen?*
How much is it_____ per page?	Wieviel kostet das pro Seite? *veefeel kostet dass pro zaiter?*

🔵 .2 Telephone

See also 1.8 Telephone alphabet

● **All phone booths** offer a direct international service to the UK. To phone the UK dial 0044, plus the UK area code without the first 0. They are either coin phones (10 Pfennig, 50 Pfennig, 1 DM, 5 DM) or card phones. The cards can be bought at post offices. Some telephone booths will also accept credit cards. Phone booths do not accept incoming calls. A reverse-charge call (*ein R-Gespräch*) has to go via the operator. When phoning someone in Germany, you may be greeted with the subscriber's name or with *Hallo* or *Ja*.

Is there a phone box _____ around here?	Ist hier eine Telefonzelle in der Nähe? *ist heer ainer telefon tseller in dayr nayher?*
Could I use your _____ phone, please?	Dürfte ich Ihr Telefon benutzen? *duerfter ikh eer telefoan benuetsen?*
Do you have a _____ (city/region)...phone directory?	Haben Sie ein Telefonbuch (von der Stadt.../ dem Bezirk...)? *harben zee ain telefoan bookh (fon dayr* *shtat.../daym betseerk...)?*
Where can I get a _____ phone card?	Wo kann ich eine Telefonkarte kaufen? *vo kann ikh ainer telefoan karter kowfen?*
Could you give me...? _____	Könnten Sie mir...geben? *koennten zee meer...gayben?*
– the number for _____ international directory enquiries	Könnten Sie mir die Nummer der Auslandsauskunft geben? *koennten zee meer dee noomer dayr* *owslantsowskoonft gayben?*
– the number of room... ___	Könnten Sie mir die Nummer von Zimmer ... geben? *koennten zee meer dee noomer fon tsimmer* *...gayben?*

– the international access code	Könnten Sie mir die internationale Nummer geben? *koennten zee meer dee inter natseeo narle noommer gayben?*
– the country code for...	Könnten Sie mir die Ländervorwahl von ... geben? *koennten zee meer dee lender forvarl fon ... gayben?*
– the trunk code for...	Könnten Sie mir die Vorwahl von ... geben? *koennten zee meer dee forvarl fon ... gayben?*
– the number of...	Könnten Sie mir die Rufnummer von ... geben? *koennten zee meer dee roofnoomer fon ... gayben?*
Could you check if this number's correct?	Könnten Sie kontrollieren, ob diese Nummer richtig ist? *koennten zee kontroleeren, op deezer noomer rikhtikh ist?*
Can I dial international direct?	Kann ich automatisch ins Ausland telefonieren? *kan ikh owtomatish ins owslant telefoaneeren?*
Do I have to go through the switchboard?	Muss ich über die Telefonistin telefonieren? *mooss ikh ueber dee telefoanisstin telefoaneeren?*
Do I have to dial '0' first?	Muss ich erst eine Null wählen? *mooss ikh erst ainer nool vaylen?*
Do I have to book my calls?	Muss ich ein Gespräch anmelden? *mooss ikh ain geshprekh anmelden?*
Could you dial this number for me, please?	Würden Sie bitte folgende Nummer für mich anrufen? *vuerden zee bitter folgender noommer fuer mikh anroofen?*
Could you put me through to.../extension..., please?	Verbinden Sie mich bitte mit.../Apparat... *fairbinden zee mikh bitter mit.../apparart...*
I'd like to place a reverse-charge call to...	Ich möchte ein R-Gespräch mit... *ikh moekhter ain air-geshprekh mit...*
What's the charge per minute?	Wieviel kostet das pro Minute? *veefeel kostet dass pro meenooter?*
Have there been any calls for me?	Hat jemand für mich angerufen? *hat yaymant fuer mikh angeroofen?*

The conversation

Hello, this is...	Guten Tag, ... hier *gooten tark, ... heer*
Who is this, please?	Mit wem spreche ich? *mit vaym shprekher ikh?*
Is this...?	Spreche ich mit...? *shprekher ikh mit...?*
I'm sorry, I've dialled the wrong number	Entschuldigung, ich habe mich verwählt *ent shool digung, ikh harber mikh fairvaylt*

I can't hear you	Ich kann Sie nicht verstehen
	ikh kann zee nikht fairshtayhen
I'd like to speak to...	Ich möchte ... sprechen
	ikh moekhter ... shprekhen
Extension..., please	Apparat ... bitte
	apparart ... bitter
Could you ask him/her to call me back?	Er/sie möchte mich bitte zurückrufen
	ayr/zee moekhter mikh bitter tsooruekh roofen
My name's... My number's...	Mein Name ist... Meine Nummer ist...
	main narmer ist... mainer noommer ist...
I'll call back tomorrow	Ich rufe ihn/sie morgen wieder an
	ikh roofer een/zee morgen veeder an

Telefon für Sie	There's a phone call for you
Sie müssen erst eine Null wählen	You have to dial '0' first
(Einen) Augenblick bitte	One moment, please
Es antwortet niemand	There's no answer
Die Nummer ist besetzt	The line's engaged
Wollen Sie warten?	Do you want to hold?
Ich verbinde	Putting you through
Sie haben die falsche Nummer (gewählt)	You've got a wrong number
Er/sie ist im Augenblick nicht da/im Haus	He's/she's not here right now
Er/sie ist...wieder zu erreichen	He'll/she'll be back...
Dies ist der Anrufbeantworter von...	This is the answering machine of...

Shopping

Shopping

10

● **Opening times:** Supermarkets and department stores are open
Monday to Friday 8.30/9 am - 5.30/6pm, on Saturdays they are usually
closed after 2 pm. However, every first Saturday of the month is a
langer Samstag (long Saturday) which means that shops stay open
until about 6pm. In many larger towns shops stay open until 8.30 pm
on a Thursday. Smaller shops may close for lunch between 12 noon
and 2 pm and on Wednesday afternoons.

Andenkenladen	Heimwerker Markt	Schuhgeschäft
souvenir shop	DIY-store	shoe shop
Antiquitäten	Kaufhaus	Schuhmacher/
antiques	department store	Schuster
Bäckerei	Konditorei	cobbler
bakery	cake shop	Second-Hand-Laden
Beleuchtung	Kosmetiksalon	second hand goods
lighting	beauty parlour	Spielzeuggeschäft
Buchhandlung	Kürschner	toy shop
bookshop	furrier	Spirituosenhandlung
Drogerie	Kurzwarenhandlung	off licence
chemist	haberdashery	Sportartikel
Einkaufszentrum	Laden	sports shop
shopping centre	shop	Süsswaren
Eisenwarengeschäft	Metzgerei	sweet shop
hardware store	butcher's	Tante-Emma-Laden
Elektrogeräte	Molkereigeschäft	corner shop
electrical appliances	dairy	Trafik
Fahrradgeschäft	Münzwäscherei	tobacconist
cycle shop	laundrette	Uhrengeschäft
Feinkost	Musikalienhandlung	clock shop/jeweller
delicatessen	music shop	Wäscherei
Fischgeschäft	Obst und Gemüse	laundry
fishmonger	greengrocer	Zoohandlung
Flohmarkt	Ökoladen	pet shop
fleamarket	health food shop	
Florist	Optiker	
florist	opticians	
Frisör	Pelze	
hairdresser	fur	
Gärtnerei	Rauchwarengeschäft	
nursery	tobacconist	
Geschäft	Raumausstat-	
shop	tung(shaus)	
Getränkemarkt	interior decorator	
drinks store	Reinigung	
Handarbeitsgeschäft	dry cleaner	
needle work and	Schallplatten-	
wool shop	geschäft	
Handlung	record shop	
dealer	Schlachter	
Haushaltswaren	butcher	
household goods	Schmuck	
	jeweller	

Shopping

🔟 .1 Shopping conversations

Where can I get...? _____	In welchem Geschäft kann ich ... bekommen?
	in velkhem gesheft kan ikh ... bekommen?
When does this shop _____ open?	Wann hat dieses Geschäft geöffnet?
	van hat deezez gesheft geoeffnet?
Could you tell me _____ where the...department is?	Können Sie mir sagen, wo die ... Abteilung ist?
	koennen zee meer zargen vo dee ... aptailoong ist?
Could you help me, _____ please? I'm looking for...	Können Sie mir bitte helfen? Ich suche...
	koennen zee meer bitter helfen? ikh zookher...
Do you sell English/ _____ American newspapers?	Verkaufen Sie englische/amerikanische Zeitungen?
	fairkowfen zee englisher/amerikarnisher tsai toongen?

Werden Sie schon bedient? _____	Are you being served?

No, I'd like... _____	Nein, ich möchte...
	nain, ikh moekhter...
I'm just looking, _____ if that's all right	Ich möchte mich nur mal umsehen
	ikh moekhter mikh noor marl oom zayhen

Sonst noch (et)was? _____	Anything else?

Yes, I'd also like... _____	Ja, bitte auch noch...
	yar, bitter owkh nokh...
No, thank you. That's all ___	Nein, danke. Das ist alles
	nain, dunker. dass ist alles
Could you show me...? ___	Können Sie mir ... zeigen?
	koennen zee meer ... tsaigen?
I'd prefer... _____	Ich möchte lieber...
	ikh moekhter leeber...
This is not what I'm _____ looking for	Das ist nicht, was ich suche
	dass ist nikht vass ikh zookher
I'll keep looking _____	Ich sehe mich erst noch mal weiter um
	ikh zayher mikh airst nokh marl vaiter oom
Do you have _____ something...?	Haben Sie nicht etwas, was...ist?
	harben zee nikht etvass, vass...ist?
– less expensive? _____	Haben Sie nicht etwas Billigeres?
	harben zee nikht etvass billigerez?
– something smaller? _____	Haben Sie nicht etwas Kleineres?
	harben zee nikht etvass klainerez?
– something larger? _____	Haben Sie nicht etwas Grösseres?
	harben zee nikht etvass groerserez?
I'll take this one _____	Ich nehme dies
	ikh naymer deez
Does it come with _____ instructions?	Ist eine Gebrauchsanweisung dabei?
	ist ainer gebrowkhs anvai zoong darbai?

Shopping

🔟

It's too expensive _____	Ich finde es zu teuer *ikh finder ez tsoo toyer*
I'll give you... _____	Ich biete Ihnen... *ikh beeter eenen...*
Could you keep this for _____ me? I'll come back for it later	Kann ich ihn/sie/es hierlassen? Ich hole ihn/sie/es nachher ab *kan ikh een/zee/es heerlassen? ikh hoaler een/zee/es nakhherr ap*
Have you got a bag _____ for me, please?	Haben Sie bitte eine Tüte für mich? *harben zee bitter ainer tueter fuer mikh?*
Could you giftwrap _____ it, please?	Könnten Sie es bitte in Geschenkpapier einpacken? *koennten zee ez bitter in geshenk papeer ainpakken?*

(Es) tut mir leid, das haben/ _____ führen wir nicht	I'm sorry, we don't have that
(Es) tut mir leid, das ist ausverkauft _____	I'm sorry, we're sold out
Tut mir leid, das kriegen wir erst... _____ wieder rein	I'm sorry, that won't be in until...
Sie können an der Kasse zahlen _____	You can pay at the cash desk
Wir nehmen keine Kreditkarten an _____	We don't accept credit cards
Wir nehmen keine Reiseschecks an _____	We don't accept traveller's cheques
Wir nehmen kein ausländisches _____ Geld/keine Fremdwährungen an	We don't accept foreign currency

10.2 Food

I'd like a hundred _____ grams of..., please	Hundert Gramm...bitte *hoondert gramm...bitter*
– five hundred grams/ _____ half a kilo of...	Fünfhundert Gramm/ein halbes Kilo/(ein Pfund) ... bitte *fuenfhoondert gramm/ain halbes keelo/(ain pfoont)...bitter*
– a kilo of... _____	Ein Kilo ... bitte *ain keelo...bitter*
Could you...it for me, _____ please?	Würden Sie es mir bitte...? *vuerden zee es meer bitter...?*
Could you slice it/ _____ dice it for me, please?	Würden Sie es mir bitte in Scheiben/Stücke/(kleine)Würfel schneiden? *vuerden zee es meer bitter in shaiben/shtueker/(klainer) vuerfel shnaiden?*
Could you grate it _____ for me, please?	Würden Sie es mir bitte reiben? *vuerden zee es meer bitter raiben?*
Can I order it? _____	Kann ich es bestellen? *kan ikh es beshtellen?*
I'll pick it up tomorrow/ _____ at...	Ich hole es morgen/um...Uhr ab *ikh hoaler es morgen/oom...oor ap*
Can you eat/drink this? _____	Kann man das essen/trinken? *kan man dass essen/trinken?*

I saw something in the ____ window. Shall I point it out?	Ich habe im Schaufenster etwas gesehen. Soll ich es Ihnen zeigen?
	ikh harber im showfenster etvass gesayhen. zoll ikh ez eenen tsaigen?
I'd like something to_____ go with this	Ich möchte gern etwas, was hierzu passt
	ikh moekhter gayrn etvass, vass heertsoo passt
Do you have shoes_____ to match this colour?	Haben Sie Schuhe in derselben Farbe wie diese hier?
	harben zee shooer in derselben farber vee deezer heer?
I'm a size...in the UK_____	In England habe ich Grösse...
	in england harber ikh groesser...
Can I try this on? _____	Darf ich dies anprobieren?
	darf ikh dees anprobeeren?
Where's the fitting room? __	Wo ist die Anprobe?
	vo ist dee anprober?
It doesn't fit_____	Es passt mir nicht
	es passt meer nikht
This is the right size _____	Das ist die richtige Grösse
	dass ist dee rikhtiger groesser
It doesn't suit me_____	Es steht mir nicht
	es shtayt meer nikht
Do you have this/_____ these in...?	Haben Sie dies/diese auch in...?
	harben zee dees/deezer owkh in...?
The heel's too high/low ____	Ich finde den Absatz zu hoch/niedrig
	ikh finder den apzats tsoo hokh/needrikh
Is this/are these _____ genuine leather?	Ist dies/sind diese aus echtem Leder?
	ist dees/zint deezer ows ekhtem layder?
I'm looking for a.., _____ for a...-year-old baby/child	Ich suche ein(en)/eine ... für ein Baby/Kind von ... Jahren
	ikh zookher ain(en)/ainer ... fuer ain baby/kint fon ... yahren
I'd like a... _____	Ich hätte gern ein(en)/eine ... aus
	ikh hetter gayrn ain(en)/ainer ... ows
– silk _____	Ich hätte gern ein(en)/eine ... aus Seide
	ikh hetter gayrn ain(en)/ainer ... ows zaider
– cotton _____	Ich hätte gern ein(en)/eine ... aus Baumwolle
	ikh hetter gayrn ain(en)/ainer ... ows bowmvoller
– woollen _____	Ich hätte gern ein(en)/eine ... aus Wolle
	ikh hetter gayrn ain(en)/ainer ... ows voller
– linen _____	Ich hätte gern ein(en)/eine ... aus Leinen
	ikh hetter gayrn ain(en)/ainer ... ows lainen
What temperature_____ can I wash it at?	Bei welcher Temperatur kann ich es waschen?
	bai velkher temperatoor kan ikh es vashen?
Will it shrink in the _____ wash?	Läuft es (in der Wäsche) ein?
	loyft es (in der wesher) ain?

Shopping

10

Chemisch reinigen	Maschinenwaschbar	Nicht bügeln
Dry clean	Machine washable	Do not iron
Handwäsche	Nass aufhängen	Nicht schleudern
Hand wash	Drip dry	Do not spin

At the cobbler

Could you mend _____ these shoes?	Können Sie diese Schuhe reparieren? *koennen zee deezer shooer repareeren?*
Could you put new _____ soles/heels on these?	Können Sie diese hier versohlen/die Absätze erneuern? *koennen zee deezer heer fairzoalen/dee apsetzer ernoyern?*
When will they be _____ ready?	Wann sind sie fertig? *vann zint zee fairtikh?*
I'd like..., please _____	Ich möchte (gern)... *ikh moekhter (gayrn)...*
– a tin of shoe polish _____	Ich möchte gern eine Dose Schuhcreme *ikh moekhter gayrn ainer doazer shookremer*
– a pair of shoelaces_____	Ich möchte gern ein Paar Schuhbänder *ikh moekhter gayrn ain par shoobender*

10 .4 Photographs and video

I'd like a film for this_____ camera, please	Ich möchte einen Film für diesen Apparat *ikh moekhter ainen film fuer deezen apparart*
– a cartridge _____	Ich möchte eine Cassette *ikh moekhter ainer kassetter*
– a one twenty-six_____ cartridge	Ich möchte eine 126er Cassette *ikh moekhter ainer ain hoondert zekhs oont tvantsiger kassetter*
– a slide film _____	Ich möchte einen Diafilm *ikh moekhter ainen diafilm*
– a film cartridge _____	Ich möchte eine Filmcassette *ikh moekhter ainer filmkassetter*
– a videotape _____	Ich möchte ein Videoband *ikh moekhter ain veedeeo bant*
colour/black and white_____	Farbe/schwarzweiss *farber/shvarts vaiss*
super eight _____	Super 8 *zooper akht*
12/24/36 exposures _____	12/24/36 Aufnahmen *tsvoelf/feer oont tsvantsikh/zekhs oont draissikh owfnarmen*
ASA/DIN number_____	ISO Wert *eessoh vayrt*
daylight film _____	(der) Tageslichtfilm *(dayr) targes likht film*
film for artificial light _____	(der) Kunstlichtfilm *(dayr) koonst likht film*

Problems

Could you load the _____ film for me, please?
Würden Sie den Film bitte für mich einlegen?
vuerden zee den film bitter fuer mikh ainlaygen?

Could you take the film _____ out for me, please?
Würden Sie bitte den Film für mich aus der Kamera nehmen?
vuerden zee bitter dayn film fuer mikh ows der kamerar naymen?

Should I replace _____ the batteries?
Muss ich die Batterien auswechseln?
mooss ikh dee battereeyen ows vekhseln?

Could you have a look _____ at my camera, please? It's not working
Könnten Sie sich bitte mal die Kamera ansehen? Sie funktioniert nicht mehr
koennten zee zikh bitter marl dee kamerar anzayhen? zee foonk tseeoneert nikht mair

The...is broken _____
Der/die/das ... ist kaputt
dayr/dee/dass ... ist kapoott

The film's jammed _____
Der Film klemmt
dayr film klemmt

The film's broken _____
Der Film ist gerissen
dayr film ist gerissen

The flash isn't working _____
Das Blitzlicht funktioniert nicht
dass blits likht foonk tseeoneert nikht

I'd like to have this film _____ developed/printed, please
Ich möchte diesen Film entwickeln/abziehen lassen
ikh moekhter deezen film entvikkeln/ap tseeyen lassen

I'd like...prints from _____ each negative
Ich möchte von jedem Negativ ... Abzüge
ikh moekhter fon yaydem negateef ... aptsueger

glossy/mat _____
glanzend/matt
glentsent/mat

7x5 _____
Sieben mal fünf
zeeben marl fuenf

I'd like to reorder _____ these photos
Ich möchte diese Fotos nachbestellen
ikh moekhter deezer fotos nakh beshtellen

I'd like to have this _____ photo enlarged
Ich möchte dieses Foto vergrössern lassen
ikh moekhter deezez foto fair groessern lassen

How much is _____ processing?
Wieviel kostet das Entwickeln?
veefeel kostet dass entvikkeln?

– printing _____
Wieviel kosten die Abzüge?
veefeel kosten dee aptsueger?

– it to reorder _____
Wieviel kostet die Nachbestellung?
veefeel kostet dee nakh beshtelloong?

– the enlargement _____
Wieviel kostet die Vergrösserung?
veefeel kostet dee fair groesseroong?

When will they _____ be ready?
Wann sind sie fertig?
vann zint zee fairtikh?

Shopping

10

10.5 At the hairdresser's

Do I have to make an appointment?	Muss ich einen Termin machen? *mooss ikh ainen termeen makhen?*
Can I come in straight away?	Kann ich sofort drankommen? *kann ikh zofort drannkommen?*
How long will I have to wait?	Wie lange muss ich warten? *vee langer mooss ikh varten?*
I'd like a shampoo/haircut	Ich möchte mir die Haare waschen/schneiden lassen *ikh moekhter meer dee haarer vashen/shnaiden lassen*
I'd like a shampoo for oily/dry hair, please	Ein Shampoo gegen fettes/trockenes Haar bitte *ain shampoo gaygen fettez/trokkenez haar bitter*
an anti-dandruff shampoo	Ein Shampoo gegen Schuppen bitte *ain shampoo gaygen shooppen bitter*
– a shampoo for permed/coloured hair	Ein Shampoo für dauergewelltes/gefärbtes Haar bitte *ain shampoo fuer dower gevelltes/gefayrptes har bitter*
– a colour rinse shampoo	Ein Farbshampoo bitte *ain farp shampoo bitter*
– a shampoo with conditioner	Ein Shampoo mit einem Pflegemittel bitte *ain shampoo mit ainem pflayger mittel bitter*
– highlights	Blonde Strähnchen bitte *blonder shtraynkhen bitter*
Do you have a colour chart, please?	Hätten Sie eine Farbenkarte? *hetten zee ainer farben karter?*
I want to keep it the same colour	Ich möchte die Farbe behalten *ikh moekhter dee farber behalten*
I'd like it darker/lighter	Ich möchte es dunkler/heller haben *ikh moekhter ez doonkler/heller harben*
I'd like/I don't want hairspray	Ich möchte (keinen) Haarfestiger *ikh moekhter (kainen) haarfestigger*
– gel	Ich möchte (kein) Gel *ikh moekhter (kain) jell*
– lotion	Ich möchte (keine) Lotion *ikh moekhter (kainer) loatseeyoan*
I'd like a short fringe	Ich möchte meinen Pony kurz tragen *ikh moekhter mainen pony koorts tragen*
Not too short at the back	Hinten nicht zu kurz schneiden bitte *hinten nikht tsoo koorts shnaiden bitter*
Not too long here	Hier bitte nicht zu lang *heer bitter nikht tsoo lang*
I'd like/I don't want (many) curls	Ich möchte (nicht zuviel) Locken *ikh moekhter (nikht tsoofeel) locken*
It needs a little/a lot taken off	Bitte schneiden Sie ein kleines bisschen/ein gutes Stück ab *bitter shnaiden zee ain klainez bisskhen/ain gootez shtook ap*
I'd like it the same as in this photo	Ich möchte eine Frisur wie auf diesem Foto *ikh moekhter ainer frizoor vee owf deezem foto*

Shopping 10

Could you put the _____ drier up/down a bit?	Könnten Sie die Haube etwas höher/niedriger einstellen?
	koennten zee dee howber etvass hoeher/needriger ain shtellen?
I'd like a facial _____	Ich möchte eine Gesichtsmaske
	ikh moekhter ainer gezikhts masker
– a manicure _____	Ich möchte mich maniküren lassen
	ikh moekhter mikh manni kueren lassen
– a massage _____	Ich möchte eine Massage

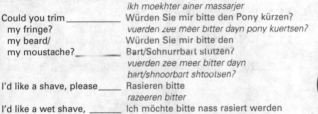

Welchen Schnitt möchten Sie? _____	How do you want it cut?
Welches Modell möchten Sie? _____	What style did you have in mind?
Welche Farbe soll es sein? _____	What colour did you want it?
Ist das die richtige Temperatur? _____	Is the temperature all right for you?
Wünschen Sie etwas zu(m) Lesen? _____	Would you like something to read?
Wünschen Sie etwas zu trinken? _____	Would you like a drink?
Ist es so richtig? _____	Is this what you had in mind?

	ikh moekhter ainer massarjer
Could you trim _____ my fringe?	Würden Sie mir bitte den Pony kürzen?
	vuerden zee meer bitter dayn pony kuertsen?
my beard/ my moustache? _____	Würden Sie mir bitte den Bart/Schnurrbart stutzen?
	vuerden zee meer bitter dayn bart/shnoorbart shtootsen?
I'd like a shave, please _____	Rasieren bitte
	razeeren bitter
I'd like a wet shave, please _____	Ich möchte bitte nass rasiert werden
	ikh moekhter bitter nass razeert verden

At the Tourist Information Centre

11 .1 **P**laces of interest

Where's the Tourist Information, please?	Wo ist der Fremdenverkehrsverein? *vo ist dayr fremden fayr kayrs fairrain?*
Do you have a city map?	Haben Sie einen Stadtplan? *harben zee ainen shtatplan?*
Could you give me some information about...?	Können Sie mir Auskunft geben über...? *koennen zee meer owskoonft gayben ueber...?*
How much is that?	Wieviel kostet das? *veefeel kostet dass?*
What are the main places of interest?	Welches sind die wichtigsten Sehenswürdigkeiten? *velkhez zint dee vikhtikhsten zayhens vuerdikh kaiten?*
Could you point them out on the map?	Könnten Sie mir die auf dem Plan zeigen? *koennten zee meer dee owf daym plam tsaigen?*
What do you recommend?	Was empfehlen Sie uns? *vass empfaylen zee oons?*
We'll be here for a few hours	Wir bleiben hier ein paar Stunden *veer blaiben heer ain par shtoonden*
– a day	Wir bleiben hier einen Tag *veer blaiben heer ainen tark*
– a week	Wir bleiben hier eine Woche *veer blaiben heer ainer vokher*
We're interested in...	Wir interessieren uns für... *veer interesseeren oons fuer...*
Is there a scenic walk around the city?	Können wir einen Stadtrundgang machen? *koennen veer ainen shtat roont gang makhen?*
How long does it take?	Wie lange dauert der? *vee langer dowert dayr?*
Where does it start/end?	Wo ist der Anfang/das Ende? *vo ist der anfang/dass ender?*
Are there any boat cruises here?	Gibt es hier Rundfahrtboote/-schiffe/Ausflugsschiffe? *gipt es heer roont fahrt boater/shiffer/-ows flooks shiffer?*
Where can we board?	Wo können wir an Bord gehen? *vo koennen veer an bort gayhen?*
Are there any bus tours?	Gibt es Busrundfahrten? *gipt es boos roont fahrten?*
Where do we get on?	Wo müssen wir einsteigen? *vo muessen veer ainshtaigen?*
Is there a guide who speaks English?	Gibt es einen englisch sprechenden Führer? *gipt ez ainen english shprekhenden fuerer?*
Are there any excursions?	Gibt es Ausflüge? *gipt ez owsflueger?*

What trips can we take around the area?	Welche Ausflüge in die Umgebung kann man machen? *velkher owsfiooger in dee oom gay boong kann man makhen?*
Where do they go to?	Wohin gehen die? *vohin gayhen dee?*
We'd like to go to...	Wir möchten nach... *veer moekhten nakh...*
How long is the trip?	Wie lange dauert der Ausflug? *vee langer dowert dayr owsflook?*
How long do we stay in...?	Wie lange bleiben wir in...? *vee langer blaiben veer in...?*
Are there any guided tours?	Gibt es Führungen? *gipt ez fyueroongen?*
How much free time will we have there?	Wieviel Freizeit haben wir da? *veefeel fraitsait harben veer dar?*
We want to go hiking	Wir möchten eine Wanderung machen *veer moekhten ainer vanderoong makhen*
Can we hire a guide?	Können wir einen Führer engagieren? *koennen veer ainen fuerer engajeeren?*
Can I book mountain huts?	Kann ich einen Platz in einer (Berg)hütte reservieren lassen? *kann ikh ainen plats in ainer (berg)hueter rezerveeren lassen?*
What time does... open/close?	Wann öffnet/schliesst (der/die/das)...? *van oeffnet/shleest (dayr/dee/dass)...?*
What days is...open/ closed?	An welchen Tagen ist der/die/das... geöffnet/geschlossen? *an velkhen targen ist dayr/dee/dass ... geoeffnet/geshlossen?*
What's the admission price?	Wieviel kostet der Eintritt? *veefeel kostet dayr aintrit?*
Is there a group discount?	Gibt es Gruppenermässigung? *gipt es groopen ermayssigoong?*
Is there a child discount?	Gibt es Ermässigung für Kinder? *gipt es ermayssigoong fuer kinder?*
Is there a discount for pensioners?	Gibt es Ermässigung für Senioren? *gipt es ermayssigoong fuer zeneeoren?*
Can I take (flash) photos/can I film here?	Darf ich hier (mit Blitzlicht) fotografieren/filmen? *darf ikh heer (mit blitslikht) foto grafeeren/filmen?*
Do you have any postcards of...?	Verkaufen Sie Ansichtskarten von dem/ der...? *fayrkowfen zee an sikhts karten fon daym/ dayr...?*
Do you have an English...?	Haben Sie ein(en)/eine ... auf englisch? *harben zee ain(en)/ainer ... owf english?*
– an English catalogue?	Haben Sie einen Katalog auf englisch? *harben zee ainen kataloak owf english?*
– an English programme?	Haben Sie ein Programm auf englisch? *harben zee ain program owf english?*
– an English brochure?	Haben Sie eine Broschüre auf englisch? *harben zee ainer broashoorer owf english?*

● **At the cinema** most films are dubbed (*synchronisiert*). In larger towns and cities as well as art cinemas subtitled versions are often screened, advertised as *Original mit Untertiteln*.

Do you have this _____ week's/month's entertainment guide?	Haben Sie den Veranstaltungskalender von dieser Woche/diesem Monat? *harben zee den fairan shtal toongs kalen der fon deezer vokher/deezem moanart?*
What's on tonight? _____	Was für Veranstaltungen gibt es heute abend? *vass fuer fairan shtal toongen gipt es hoyter arbent?*
We want to go to... _____	Wir möchten in den/ins/in die... *veer moekhten in dayn/ins/in dee...*
Which films are _____ showing?	Welche Filme werden gespielt? *velkher filmer vairden geshpeelt?*
What sort of film is that?___	Was für ein Film ist das? *vass fuer ain film ist dass?*
rated suitable for _____ the whole family	für jedes Alter *fuer yaydez alter*
rated not suitable for _____ children under 12/16 years	ab 12/16 Jahre(n) *ap tsvoelf/zekh tsayn yahre(n)*
original version _____	Originalfassung *origginaal fassoong*
subtitled_____	untertitelt *oonter teetelt*
dubbed _____	synchronisiert *suen khro nee zeert*
Is it a continuous_____ showing?	Ist es eine durchgehende Vorführung? *ist es ainer doorkh gayhender for fue roong?*
What's on at...? _____	Was gibt es in...? *vass gipt es in...?*
– the theatre? _____	Was gibt es im Theater? *vass gipt es im tayarter?*
– the concert hall? _____	Was gibt es in der Konzerthalle/im Konzertsaal? *vass gipt es in dayr kontsert haller/im kontsert zarl?*
– the opera? _____	Was gibt es in der Oper? *vass gipt es in dayr oaper?*
Where can I find a good ___ disco around here?	Wo gibt es hier eine gute Disko? *vo gipt es heer ainer gooter disko?*
Is it members only? _____	Muss man Mitglied sein? *mooss man mittgleet zain?*
Where can I find a good ___ nightclub around here?	Wo gibt es einen guten Nachtklub? *vo gipt es ainen gooten nakht kloop?*
Is it evening wear only? ___	Ist Abendkleidung Zwang? *ist arbent klai doong tsvang?*
Should I/we dress up? _____	Ist Abendkleidung erwünscht? *ist arbent klai doong errvuensht?*
What time does the _____ show start?	Wann beginnt die Show? *vann begint dee shoa?*

When's the next soccer match?	Wann ist das nächste Fussballspiel?
	van ist dass nekster foos barl shpeel?
Who's playing?	Wer spielt gegen wen?
	vayr shpeelt gaygen vayn?
I'd like a _____ female/male escort for tonight. Could you arrange that for me?	Ich möchte für heute abend weibliche/männliche Begleitung. Können Sie mir die besorgen?
	ikh moekhter fuer hoyter arbent vai plikher/mennlikher beglaitung. koennen zee meer dee bezorgen?

.3 Booking tickets

Could you book some tickets for us?	Können Sie für uns reservieren?
	koennen zee fuer oons rezerveeren?
We'd like to book... seats/a table...	Wir möchten...Plätze/einen Tisch...reservieren
	veer moekhten...pletzer/ainen tish...rezerveeren
– in the stalls	Wir möchten...Plätze/einen Tisch im Parkett reservieren
	veer moekhten...pletzer/ainen tish im parkett rezerveeren
– on the balcony	Wir möchten...Balkonplätze/einen Tisch auf dem Balkon reservieren
	veer moekhten...balkoanpletzer/ainen tish owf daym balkoan rezerveeren
– box seats	Wir möchten...Logenplätze reservieren
	veer moekhten...loagen pletzer rezerveeren
– seats at the front	Bitte Plätze vorn
	bitter pletser forn
– seats in the middle	Bitte Plätze in der Mitte
	bitter pletser in der mitter
– seats at the back	Bitte Plätze hinten
	bitter pletser hinten
Could I book...seats for the...o'clock performance?	Kann ich...Plätze für die Vorstellung von...Uhr reservieren lassen?
	kan ikh...pletser fuer dee for shtel loong fon ...oohr rezerveeren lassen?
Are there any seats left for tonight?	Gibt es noch Karten für heute abend?
	gipt es nokh karten fuer hoyter arbent?
How much is a ticket?	Wieviel kostet eine Karte?
	veefeel kostet ainer karter?
When can I pick the tickets up?	Wann kann ich die Karten abholen?
	van kan ikh dee karten aphoalen?
I've got a reservation	Ich habe reserviert
	ikh harber rezerveet
My name's...	Mein Name ist...
	main narmer ist...

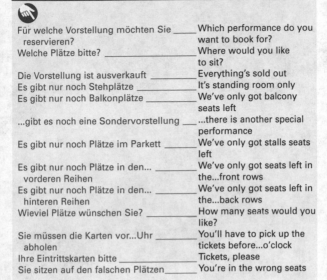

Für welche Vorstellung möchten Sie reservieren?	Which performance do you want to book for?
Welche Plätze bitte?	Where would you like to sit?
Die Vorstellung ist ausverkauft	Everything's sold out
Es gibt nur noch Stehplätze	It's standing room only
Es gibt nur noch Balkonplätze	We've only got balcony seats left
...gibt es noch eine Sondervorstellung	...there is another special performance
Es gibt nur noch Plätze im Parkett	We've only got stalls seats left
Es gibt nur noch Plätze in den... vorderen Reihen	We've only got seats left in the...front rows
Es gibt nur noch Plätze in den... hinteren Reihen	We've only got seats left in the...back rows
Wieviel Plätze wünschen Sie?	How many seats would you like?
Sie müssen die Karten vor...Uhr abholen	You'll have to pick up the tickets before...o'clock
Ihre Eintrittskarten bitte	Tickets, please
Sie sitzen auf den falschen Plätzen	You're in the wrong seats

Sports

12 Sports

12 .1 Sporting questions

Where can we... around here?	Wo können wir hier...?
	vo koennen veer heer...?
Is there a... around here?	Gibt es hier in der Nähe ein(en)/eine...?
	gipt es heer in dayr nayher ain(en)/ainer...?
Can I hire a...here?	Kann ich hier ein(en)/eine...mieten/leihen?
	kan ikh heer ain(en)/ainer...meeten/laihen?
Can I take...lessons?	Kann ich ...Stunden nehmen?
	kan ikh ... shtoonden naymen?
How much is that per hour/per day/a turn?	Wieviel kostet das pro Stunde/Tag/Mal?
	veefeel kostet dass pro shtoonder/tark/marl?
Do I need a permit for that?	Braucht man dafür einen Schein/eine Genehmigung?
	browkht man darfuer ainen shain/ainer genay mi goong?
Where can I get the permit?	Wo kann ich die Genehmigung bekommen?
	vo kan ikh dee genay mi goong bekommen?

12 .2 By the waterfront

Is it a long way to the sea still?	Ist es noch weit bis ans Meer?
	ist es nokh vait biss ans meer?
Is there a...around here?	Gibt es hier in der Nähe ein... ?
	gipt es heer in dayr nayher ain... ?
-an outdoor/indoor/ public swimming pool	Gibt es hier in der Nähe ein (openair pool) Freibad/(indoor pool) Hallenbad/(public pool) eine Badeanstalt?
	gipt es heer in dayr nayher ain fraibart/ainer hallen bart/ainer barder an shalt/?
– a sandy beach	Gibt es hier in der Nähe einen Sandstrand?
	gipt ez heer in dayr nayher ainen sant shtrant?
– a nudist beach	Gibt es hier in der Nähe einen Nacktbadestrand?
	gipt ez heer in dayr nayher ainen nakt barder shtrant?
– mooring	Gibt es hier in der Nähe einen Anlegeplatz?
	gipt ez heer in dayr nayher ainen anlayger plats?
Are there any rocks here?	Sind hier Felsen?
	zint heer felzen?
When's high/low tide?	Wann ist Flut/Ebbe?
	van ist floot/ebber?
What's the water temperature?	Welche Temperatur hat das Wasser?
	velkher temperatoor hat dass vasser?
Is it (very) deep here?	Ist es hier (sehr) tief?
	ist ez heer (zayr) teef?
Can you stand here?	Kann man hier stehen?
	kan man heer shtayen?
Is it safe to swim here?	Kann man/(können Kinder) hier ungefährdet schwimmen?
	kan man/(koennen kinder) heer ungefayrdet shvimmen?
Are there any currents?	Gibt es Strömungen?
	gipt ez shtroe moongen?

Are there any rapids/ waterfalls in this river?	Hat dieser Fluss Stromschnellen/Wasserfälle?	*hat deezer flooss shtrom shnellen/vasser feller?*
What does that flag/ buoy mean?	Was bedeutet die Flagge/Boje dort?	*vass bedoytet dee flagger/boayer dort?*
Is there a life guard on duty here?	Gibt es hier einen Bademeister, der aufpasst?	*gipt es heer ainen barder maister, der owfpasst?*
Are dogs allowed here?	Sind hier Hunde erlaubt?	*zint heer hoonder erlowpt?*
Is camping on the beach allowed?	Darf man hier am Strand campen?	*darf man heer am shtrant kampen?*
Are we allowed to build a fire here?	Darf man hier Feuer machen?	*darf man heer foyer makhen?*

Achtung! Gefahr! Danger	Angeln verboten No fishing	Nur mit Genehmigung Permits only
Angeln erlaubt Fishing water	Baden verboten No swimming	Surfen verboten No surfing

12.3 In the snow

Can I take ski lessons here?	Kann ich hier Skistunden nehmen?	*kan ikh heer shee shtoonden naymen?*
for beginners/advanced	für Anfänger/(etwas) Fortgeschrittene	*fuer anfenger/(etvass) fortgeshrittenner*
How large are the groups?	Wie gross sind die Gruppen?	*vee groass zint dee grooppen?*
What language are the classes in?	In welcher Sprache werden die Stunden gegeben?	*in velkher shprakher verden dee shtoonden gegayben?*
I'd like a lift pass, please	Ich möchte einen Ski(lift)pass	*ikh moekhter ainen shee(lift)pass*
Must I give you a passport photo?	Muss ich ein Passbild abgeben?	*mooss ikh ain passbilt apgayben?*
Where can I have a passport photo taken?	Wo kann ich ein Passbild machen lassen?	*vo kan ikh ain passbilt makhen lassen?*
Where are the beginners' slopes?	Wo sind die Skipisten für Anfänger? (jokey): Wo ist der Idiotenhügel?)	*vo zint dee shee pisten fuer anfenger?* *vo ist dayr eedeeeoa ten huegel?*
Are there any runs for cross-country skiing?	Gibt es hier in der Nähe Loipen?	*gipt ez heer in dayr nayher loypen?*
Have the cross-country runs been marked?	Sind die Loipen beschildert?	*zint dee loypen beshildert?*
Are the...in operation?	Sind die...geöffnet?	*zint dee...geoeffnet?*
– the ski lifts	Sind die Skilifte geöffnet?	*zint dee sheelifter geoeffnet?*
– the chair lifts	Sind die Sessellifte geöffnet?	*zint dee zessel lifter geoeffnet?*
Are the slopes usable?	Sind die Pisten offen?	*zint dee pisten offen?*
Are the cross-country runs usable?	Sind die Loipen offen?	*zint dee loypen offen?*

Sickness

13 Sickness

13.1 Call (fetch) the doctor

Could you call/fetch a_____ doctor quickly, please?	Rufen/holen Sie bitte schnell einen Arzt *roofen/hoalen zee bitter shnell ainen artst*
When does the doctor _____ have surgery?	Wann hat der Arzt Sprechstunde? *van hat dayr artst shprekh shtoonder?*
When can the doctor _____ come?	Wann kann der Arzt kommen? *van kan dayr artst kommen?*
I'd like to make an_____ appointment to see the doctor	Können Sie für mich einen Termin beim Arzt machen? *koennen zee fuer mikh ainen tairmeen baim artst makhen?*
I've got an appointment _____ to see the doctor at...	Ich habe um...Uhr einen Termin beim Arzt *ikh harber oom...ooer ainen tairmeen baim artst*
Which doctor/chemist _____ has night/weekend duty?	Welcher Arzt/welche Apotheke hat Nachtdienst/Notdienst? *velkher artst/velkher apotayker hat nakht deenst/noat deenst?*

13.2 Patient's ailments

I don't feel well _____	Ich fühle mich unwohl *ikh fueler mikh oonvoal*
I'm dizzy_____	Mir ist schwindlig *meer ist shvindlikh*
– ill_____	Ich bin krank *ikh bin krank*
– sick_____	Mir ist schlecht/übel *meer ist shlekht/uebel*
I've got a cold_____	Ich bin erkältet *ikh bin erkelltet*
It hurts here _____	Ich habe hier Schmerzen *ikh harber heer shmertsen*
I've been throwing up _____	Ich habe mich übergeben *ikh harber mikh uebergayben*
I've got... _____	Ich habe...Beschwerden *ikh harber...beshverden*
I'm running a _____ temperature of...degrees	Ich habe...(Grad) Fieber *ikh harber...(grart) feeber*
I've been stung by_____ a wasp	Ich bin von einer Wespe gestochen worden *ikh bin fon ainer vesper geshtokhen vorden*
I've been stung by an_____ insect	Ein Insekt hat mich gestochen oder gebissen *ain inzekt hat mikh geshtokhen oader gebissen*
I've been bitten by _____ a dog	Mich hat ein Hund gebissen *mikh hat ain hoont gebissen*
I've been stung by_____ a jellyfish	Mich hat eine Qualle gestochen *mikh hat ainer kvaller geshtokhen*
I've been bitten by _____ a snake	Mich hat eine Schlange gebissen *mikh hat ainer shlanger gebissen*

I've been bitten by _____ an animal	Mich hat ein Tier gebissen
	mikh hat ain teer gebissen
I've cut myself _____	Ich habe mich geschnitten
	ikh harber mikh geshnitten
I've burned myself _____	Ich habe mich verbrannt
	ikh harber mikh fayrbrant
I've grazed myself _____	Ich habe eine Hautabschürfung
	ikh harber ainer howt ap shuer foong
I've had a fall _____	Ich bin gestürzt
	ikh bin geshtuertst
I've sprained my ankle _____	Ich habe mir den Knöchel verstaucht
	ikh harber meer den knoekhel fairshtowkht
I've come for the _____ morning-after pill	Ich möchte die 'Pille danach'
	ikh moekhter dee 'piller darnakh'

13.3 The consultation

Was für Beschwerden haben Sie? _____ (Wo fehlt's denn?)	What seems to be the problem?
Wie lange haben Sie diese _____ Beschwerden schon?	How long have you had these symptoms?
Haben Sie diese Beschwerden schon _____ früher gehabt?	Have you had this trouble before?
Wie hoch ist das Fieber? _____	How high is your temperature?
Machen Sie sich bitte frei _____	Get undressed, please
Machen Sie bitte den Oberkörper frei _____	Strip to the waist, please
Sie können sich dort _____ ausziehen/freimachen	You can undress there
Bitte machen Sie den linken/rechten _____ Arm frei	Roll up your left/right sleeve, please
Legen Sie sich hierauf _____	Lie down here, please
Tut das weh?/Haben Sie hier _____ Schmerzen?	Does this hurt?
Tief ein- und ausatmen _____	Breathe deeply
Öffnen Sie den Mund _____	Open your mouth

Patient's medical history

I'm a diabetic _____	Ich bin zuckerkrank/Diabetiker
	ikh bin tsooker krank/deea bayt ikker
I have a heart condition _____	Ich bin herzkrank/Ich habe ein Herzleiden
	ikh bin hairtskrank/ikh harber ain hertslaiden
I have asthma _____	Ich habe Asthma/Ich bin Asthmatiker
	ikh harber astmar/ikh bin astmartikker
I'm allergic to... _____	Ich bin allergisch gegen...
	ikh bin allairgish gaygen...
I'm...months pregnant _____	Ich bin...Monate schwanger
	ikh bin...moanarter shvanger
I'm on a diet _____	Ich habe eine Diät
	ikh harber ainer deeyayt
I'm on medication/the pill _____	Ich nehme Medikamente/die Pille
	ikh naymer medee ker menter/dee piller

I've had a heart attack once before	Ich habe schon mal einen Herzanfall gehabt
	ikh harber shoan mall ainen hertsanfall gehapt
I've had a(n)...operation	Ich bin am/an der...operiert
	ikh bin am/an dayr...opereert
I've been ill recently	Ich bin gerade krank gewesen
	ikh bin gerarder krank gevayzen
I've got an ulcer	Ich habe ein Magengeschwür
	ikh harber ain margen geshvuer
I've got my period	Ich habe meine Periode
	ikh harber mainer peree oader

Sind Sie gegen irgendetwas allergisch?	Do you have any allergies?
Nehmen Sie Medikamente (ein)?	Are you on any medication?
Haben Sie eine Diät?	Are you on a diet?
Sind Sie schwanger?	Are you pregnant?
Sind Sie gegen Wundstarrkrampf geimpft?	Have you had a tetanus injection?

Es ist nichts Ernstes	It's nothing serious
Sie haben sich den/die/das... gebrochen	Your...is broken
Sie haben sich den/die/das... verstaucht	You've sprained...
Sie haben einen Riss...	You've got (a) torn...
Sie haben eine Entzündung	You've got an inflammation
Sie haben Blinddarmentzündung	You've got appendicitis
Sie haben Bronchitis	You've got bronchitis
Sie haben eine Geschlechtskrankheit	You've got a venereal disease
Sie haben Grippe	You've got the flu
Sie haben einen Herzanfall gehabt	You've had a heart attack
Sie haben eine Infektion (Virus, bakterielle)	You've got an infection (viral, bacterial)
Sie haben Lungenentzündung	You've got pneumonia
Sie haben ein Magengeschwür	You've got an ulcer
Sie haben eine Muskelzerrung	You've pulled a muscle
Sie haben eine vaginale Entzündung	You've got a vaginal infection
Sie haben eine Lebensmittelvergiftung/Nahrungs-mittelvergiftung	You've got food poisoning
Sie haben einen Sonnenstich	You've got sunstroke
Sie sind allergisch gegen...	You're allergic to...
Sie sind schwanger	You're pregnant

Sickness

13

Ich möchte eine_____ Blut/Harn/Stuhluntersuchung machen lassen	I'd like to have your blood/urine/stools tested
Es muss genäht werden _____	It needs stitching
Ich schicke Sie zu einem Facharzt/ins____ Krankenhaus/Hospital	I'm referring you to a specialist/sending you to hospital.
Es müssen Röntgenaufnahmen gemacht werden _____	You'll need to have some x-rays taken
Setzen Sie sich bitte (wieder) ins_____ Wartezimmer_____	Could you wait in the waiting room, please?
Sie müssen operiert werden _____	You'll need an operation

The diagnosis

Is it contagious?_____	Ist es ansteckend?
	ist ez anshtekkent?
How long do I have to ____ stay...?	Wie lange muss ich...bleiben?
	vee langer mooss ikh...blaiben?
– in bed _____	Wie lange muss ich im Bett bleiben?
	vee langer mooss ikh im bett blaiben?
– in hospital _____	Wie lange muss ich im Krankenhaus bleiben?
	vee langer mooss ikh im kranken howz blaiben?
Do I have to go on _____ a special diet?	Muss ich eine Diät einhalten?
	mooss ikh ainer deeyayt ainhalten?
Am I allowed to travel? ____	Darf ich reisen?
	darf ikh raizen?
Can I make a new _____ appointment?	Kann ich einen neuen Termin machen?
	kan ikh ainen noyen termeen makhen?
When do I have to_____ come back?	Wann soll ich wiederkommen?
	van zoll ikh veeder kommen?
I'll come back _____ tomorrow	Ich komme morgen wieder
	ikh kommer morgen veeder

Kommen Sie morgen/in ... _____ Tagen wieder	Come back tomorrow/in...days' time.

13 .4 Medication and prescriptions

How do I take this _____ medicine?	Wie soll ich diese Medikamente einnehmen?
	vee zoll ikh deezer medee kar menter ain naymen?
How many capsules/ _____ drops/injections/spoon- fuls/tablets each time?	Wieviel Kapseln/Tropfen/Spritzen/Löffel/ Tabletten/Zäpfchen pro Mal?
	veefeel kapseln/tropfen/shpritsen/loeffel/ tabletten/tsepfkhen pro marl?
How many times a day? ___	Wie oft täglich?
	vee oft tayglikh?

I've forgotten my ___ medication. At home I take...	Ich habe meine Medikamente vergessen. Zu hause nehme ich...
	ikh harber mainer medee kar menter fairgessen. tsoo howzer naymer ikh...
Could you make out a ___ prescription for me?	Können Sie mir ein Rezept ausstellen?
	koennen zee meer ain retsept ows shtellen?

Ich verschreibe Ihnen ein ___ Antibiotikum/einen Saft/ein Beruhigungsmittel/Schmerzmittel	I'm prescribing antibiotics/a mixture/a tranquillizer/pain killers
Sie dürfen sich nicht anstrengen/Sie ___ müssen sich schonen	Have lots of rest
Sie dürfen nicht nach draussen ___	Stay indoors
Sie müssen im Bett bleiben ___	Stay in bed

alle...Stunden every...hours	Kapseln capsules	Spritzen injections
die Kur beenden finish the course	Löffel (Ess-/Tee-) spoonfuls	Tabletten tablets
dieses Medikament beeinträchtigt die Fahrtüchtigkeit this medication impairs your driving	(tablespoons/ teaspoons)	Tropfen drops
	...mal täglich ...times a day	vor jeder Mahlzeit before meals
einnehmen take	nicht zerkauen do not chew	während...Tagen for...days
einreiben rub on	nur für äusserliche Anwendung for external use only	Zäpfchen suppository
in Wasser (auf)lösen dissolve in water	Salbe ointment	

13.5 At the dentist's

Do you know a good ___ dentist?	Können Sie mir einen guten Zahnarzt/Dentisten empfehlen?
	koennen zee meer ainen gooten tsarn artst/denteesten empfaylen?
Could you make a ___ dentist's appointment for me? It's urgent	Können Sie mir einen Termin beim Zahnarzt besorgen? Es eilt
	koennen zee meer ainen termeen baim tsarn artst bezorgen? Ez ailt
Can I come in today, ___ please?	Könnte ich bitte heute noch kommen?
	koennter ikh bitter hoyter nokh kommen?
I have (terrible) ___ toothache	Ich habe (schreckliche) Zahnschmerzen
	ikh harber (shrek likher) tsarn shmertsen

Could you prescribe/ give me a painkiller?	Können Sie mir ein Schmerzmittel verschreiben/geben?
	koennen zee meer ain shmairts mittel fairshraiben/gayben?
A piece of my tooth/ molar has broken off	Mir ist ein Stück vom Zahn/Backenzahn abgebrochen
	meer ist ain shtuek fom tsarn/bakkentsarn apgebrokhen
My filling's come out	Ich habe eine Füllung verloren
	ikh harber ainer fuellung fairloren
I've got a broken crown	Mir ist eine Krone abgebrochen
	meer ist ainer kroner apgebrokhen
I'd like/I don't want a local anaesthetic	Ich möchte (nicht) örtlich betäubt werden
	ikh moekhter (nikht) oertlikh betoypt verden
Can you do a makeshift repair job?	Können Sie mir jetzt provisorisch helfen?
	koennen zee meer yetst provee zorish helfen?
I don't want this tooth pulled	Ich will nicht, dass dieser Zahn gezogen wird
	ikh vill nikht, dass deezer tsarn getsoagen virt
My dentures are broken. Can you fix them?	Mein Gebiss ist zerbrochen. Können Sie es reparieren?
	main gebiss ist tsayrbrokhen. koennen zee es repareeren?

Welcher Zahn/(Backenzahn) tut weh?	Which tooth hurts?
Sie haben ein(en) Abszess	You've got an abscess
Ich muss eine Nervenbehandlung machen/durchführen	I'll have to do a root canal
Ich betäube Sie örtlich	I'm giving you a local anaesthetic
Ich muss diesen... füllen/ziehen/abschleifen	I'll have to fill/pull/file this tooth
Ich muss bohren	I'll have to drill
Mund auf, bitte	Open wide, please
Mund zu,bitte	Close your mouth, please

Sickness

13

14 In trouble

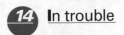

14 In trouble

14.1 Asking for help

Help!	Hilfe! *hillfer!*
Fire!	Feuer! *foyer!*
Police!	Polizei! *poleetsai!*
Quick!	Schnell! *shnell!*
Danger!	Gefahr! *gefahr!*
Watch out!	Achtung! *akhtoong!*
Stop!	Halt! *halt!*
Be careful!	Vorsicht! *forzikht!*
Don't!	Nicht tun! *nikht toon!*
Let go!	Loslassen! *loaslassen!*
Stop that thief!	Haltet den Dieb! *haltet den deep!*
Could you help me, please?	Würden Sie mir bitte helfen? *vuerden zee meer bitter helfen?*
Where's the police station/emergency exit/fire escape?	Wo ist die Polizeiwache/der Notausgang/die Feuertreppe? *vo ist dee polee tsai vakher/der noat ows gang/dee foyer trepper?*
Where's the fire extinguisher?	Wo ist ein Feuerlöscher? *vo ist ain foyer loesher?*
Call the fire brigade!	Rufen Sie die Feuerwehr! *roofen zee dee foyer vair!*
Call the police!	Rufen Sie die Polizei (an) *roofen zee dee poleetsai (an)*
Call an ambulance!	Rufen Sie einen Krankenwagen/Rettungswagen *roofen zee ainen krunken vargen/rettoongs vargen*
Where's the nearest phone?	Wo gibt's ein Telefon? *vo gipt's ain telefoan?*
Could I use your phone?	Darf ich Ihr Telefon benutzen? *darf ikh eer telefoan benootsen?*
What's the emergency number?	Wie lautet die Alarmnummer? *vee lowtet dee alarm noomer?*
What's the number for the police?	Wie ist die Telefonnummer der Polizei? *vee ist dee telefoan noomer dayr poleetsai?*

In trouble

14

14 .2 Loss

I've lost my purse/_____ wallet	Ich habe mein Portemonnaie/meine Brieftasche verloren
	ikh harber main portmonnay/mainer breeftasher fairloren
I left my...yesterday _____	Ich habe gestern mein(en)/meine... vergessen
	ikh harber gestern main(en)/mainer... fairgessen
I left my...here _____	Ich habe hier mein(en)/meine... liegengelassen/stehengelassen
	ikh harber heer main(en)/mainer...leegen gelassen/shtayen gelassen
Did you find my...? _____	Haben Sie mein(en)/meine...gefunden?
	harben zee main(en)/mainer...gefoonden?
It was right here_____	Er/sie/es stand/lag hier
	er/zee/es shtant/lark heer
It's quite valuable _____	Es ist sehr wertvoll
	ez ist zayr vayrtfoll
Where's the lost_____ property office?	Wo ist das Fundbüro?
	vo ist dass funt buero?

14 .3 Accidents

There's been an accident __	Es ist ein Unfall passiert
	ez ist ain unfarl passeert
Someone's fallen into _____ the water	Jemand ist ins Wasser gefallen
	yaymant ist ins vasser gefallen
There's a fire_____	Es brennt
	ez brennt
Is anyone hurt? _____	Ist jemand verletzt?
	ist yaymant fairletst?
Some people have _____ been/no one's been injured	Es gibt (keine) Verletzte(n)
	ez gipt (kainer) fairletste(n)
There's someone in _____ the car/train still	Es ist noch jemand im Auto/Zug
	ez ist nokh yaymant im owto/tsook
It's not too bad. Don't_____ worry	Es ist nicht so schlimm. Machen Sie sich keine Sorgen
	ez ist nikht zo shlimm. makhen zee zikh kainer zorgen
Leave everything the _____ way it is, please	Lassen Sie bitte alles, so wie es ist
	lassen zee bitter alles, zo vee ez ist
I want to talk to the_____ police first	Ich will erst mit der Polizei sprechen
	ikh vill airst mit dayr poleetsai shprekhen
I want to take a _____ photo first	Ich will erst ein Foto machen
	ikh vill airst ain foto makhen
Here's my name_____ and address	Hier sind mein Name und meine Adresse
	heer zint main narmer unt mainer adresser
Could I have your _____ name and address?	Geben Sie mir bitte Ihren Namen und Ihre Adresse
	gayben zee meer bitter eeren narmen unt eerer adresser

In trouble

14

Could I see some_____ identification/your insurance papers?	Dürfte ich Ihren Ausweis/Ihre Versicherungspapiere sehen? *duerfter ikh eeren owsvais/eerer fairzikheroongs papeerer zayhen?*
Will you act as a _____ witness?	Wollen Sie Zeuge sein? *vollen zee tsoyger zain?*
I need the details for _____ the insurance	Ich brauche die Angaben für die Versicherung *ikh browkher dee angarben fuer dee fair zikhe roong*
Are you insured?_____	Sind Sie versichert? *zint zee fairzikhert?*
Third party or_____ comprehensive?	Haftpflicht oder Vollkasko-Versicherung? *haftpflikht oader follkasko-fairzikhe roong?*
Could you sign here, _____ please?	Unterschreiben Sie hier bitte *oonter shraiben zee heer bitter*

14.4 Theft

I've been robbed _____	Ich bin bestohlen worden *ikh bin beshtoalen vorden*
My...has been stolen _____	Mein(e) ... ist gestohlen worden *main(er) ... ist geshtoalen vorden*
My car's been_____ broken into	Mein Auto ist aufgebrochen worden *main owto ist owfgebrokhen vorden*

14.5 Missing person

I've lost my child/_____ grandmother	Mein Kind/meine Oma ist verschwunden *main kint/mainer oamar ist fairshvoonden*
Could you help me _____ find him/her?	Würden Sie mir bitte suchen helfen? *vuerden zee meer bitter zookhen helfen?*
Have you seen a _____ small child?	Haben Sie ein kleines Kind gesehen? *harben zee ain klaines kint gezayhen?*
He's/she's...years old _____	Er/sie ist...Jahre *er/zee ist...yahrer*
He's/she's got _____ short/long/blond/red/ brown/black/grey/curly/ straight/frizzy hair	Er/sie hat kurzes/langes/blondes/rotes/braunes/ schwarzes/graues/lockiges/glattes/gekräu seltes Haar *er/zee hat koortses/langes/blondes/roates/ brownes/shvartses/growes/lokiges/glattes/ gekroyzeltes har*
with a ponytail_____	mit Pferdeschwanz *mit pferder shvants*
with plaits _____	mit Zöpfen *mit tsoepfen*
in a bun _____	mit einem Knoten/Dutt *mit ainem knooten/doott*
He's/she's got _____ blue/brown/green eyes	Die Augen sind blau/braun/grün *dee owgen zint blow/brown/gruen*
He's wearing swimming ___ trunks/mountaineering boots	Er trägt eine Badehose/Wanderschuhe *er traykht ainer barder hoazer/vander shooer*

In trouble

14

with/without glasses/ _____	mit/ohne Brille
	mit/oaner briller
tall/short _____	gross/klein
	groass/klain
This is a photo of _____ him/her	Hier ist ein Bild von ihm/ihr
	heer ist ain bilt fon eem/eer
He/she must be lost _____	Er/sie hat sich sicher verlaufen
	er/zee hat zikh zikher fairlowfen

14 .6 The police

An arrest

Ihre Fahrzeugpapiere bitte _____	Your registration papers, please
Sie sind zu schnell gefahren _____	You were speeding
Sie parken falsch _____	You're not allowed to park here
Sie haben kein Geld in die Parkuhr _____ gesteckt	You haven't put money in the meter
Ihr Licht brennt nicht _____	Your lights aren't working
Sie bekommen eine gebühren- _____ pflichtige Verwarnung/einen Strafzettel von...	You are to receive a fine of/a parking ticket for...
Zahlen Sie sofort? _____	Do you want to pay on the spot?
Sie müssen sofort bezahlen _____	You'll have to pay on the spot

---

I don't speak German _____	Ich spreche kein Deutsch
	ikh shprekher kain doytsh
I didn't see the sign _____	Ich habe das Schild nicht gesehen
	ikh harber das shilt nikht gezayhen
I don't understand _____ what it says	Ich verstehe nicht, was da steht
	ikh fairshtayher nikht, vass dar shtayt
I was only doing... _____ kilometres an hour	Ich bin nur...Kilometer pro Stunde gefahren
	ikh bin noor...keelomayter pro shtoonder gefahren
I'll have my car checked _____	Ich werde mein Auto nachsehen lassen
	ikh verder main owto nakh zayhen lassen
I was blinded by _____ oncoming lights	Der Gegenverkehr hat mich geblendet
	dayr gaygen fairkair hat mikh geblendet

At the police station

Wo ist es passiert? _____	Where did it happen?
Was haben Sie verloren? _____	What's missing?
Was ist gestohlen (worden)? _____	What's been taken?
Ihren Ausweis bitte _____	Could I see some identification?
Wann ist es passiert? _____	What time did it happen?
Wer war daran beteiligt? _____	Who was involved?
Gibt es Zeugen? _____	Are there any witnesses?
Bitte füllen Sie das aus _____	Fill this out, please
Hier bitte unterschreiben _____	Sign here, please
Möchten Sie einen Dolmetscher? _____	Do you want an interpreter?

I want to report a_____ collision/something missing/rape/missing person	Ich möchte einen Zusammenstoss/einen (things missing)Verlust/eine Vergewaltigung anzeigen/(persons missing) Ich möchte eine Vermisstenanzeige machen *ikh moekhter ainen tsoo zammen shtoas/ainen fairloost/ainer fair gevalti goong an tsaigen/ikh moekhter ainer fayrmissten antsaiger makhen*
Could you make out _____ a report, please?	Würden Sie bitte ein Protokoll aufnehmen? *vuerden zee bitter ain proatoakoll owfnaymen?*
Could I have a copy _____ for the insurance?	Geben Sie mir bitte eine Abschrift für die Versicherung *gayben zee meer bitter ainer apshrift fuer dee fair zeekhe roong*
I've lost everything _____	Ich habe alles verloren *ikh harber alles fairloren*
All my money is gone, I don't know what to do ___	Mein Geld ist alle, ich bin ratlos *main gelt ist aller, ikh bin rartloas*
Could you please lend me some?	Könnten Sie mir bitte etwas leihen? *koennten zee meer bitter etvass laihen?*
I'd like an interpreter _____	Ich möchte einen Dolmetscher *ikh moekhter ainen dolmetsher*
I'm innocent _____	Ich bin unschuldig *ikh bin oonshuldikh*
I don't know anything _____ about it	Ich weiss von nichts *ikh vaiss fon nikhts*
I want to speak to _____ someone from the British consulate	Ich möchte jemanden vom britischen Konsulat sprechen *ikh moekhter yaymanden fom breetishen konsoolart shprekhen*
I need to see someone _____ from the British embassy	Ich möchte jemanden von der breetischen Botschaft sprechen *ikh moekhter yaymunden fon dayr british boatshaft shprekhen*
I want a lawyer who _____ speaks...	Ich will einen Rechtsanwalt, der...spricht *ikh vill ainen rekhts anvalt, dayr...shprikht*

In trouble

14

15

Word list

Word list English - German

● **This word list** is meant to supplement the previous chapters. Nouns are always accompanied by the German definite article in order to indicate whether it is a masculine (*der*), feminine (*die*), or a neuter (*das*), word. In a number of cases, words not contained in this list can be found elsewhere in this book, namely alongside the diagrams of the car, the bicycle and the tent. Many food terms can be found in the German-English list in Section 4.7.

A

about	ungefähr	*oongefayr*
above	über	*ueber*
abroad	das Ausland	*dass owslant*
accident	der Unfall	*dayr oonfarl*
adder	die Natter	*dee natter*
addition	die Addition	*dee adittseeyoan*
address	die Adresse	*dee adresser*
admission	der Eintritt	*dayr aintritt*
admission price	der Eintrittspreis	*dayr aintritts praiss*
advice	der Rat	*dayr rart*
after	nach	*nakh*
afternoon	mittags	*mittargs*
aftershave	die After-shave-Lotion	*dee after-shave loatseeyown*
again	erneut	*ayrnoyt*
against	gegen	*gaygen*
age	das Alter	*dass alter*
Aids	(das) Aids	*(dass) aids*
air conditioning	die Klimaanlage	*dee kleemar anlarger*
air mattress	die Luftmatratze	*dee looft mattratser*
air sickness bag	die Spucktüte	*dee shpook tueter*
aircraft	das Flugzeug	*dass flooktsoyk*
airport	der Flughafen	*dayr flookharfen*
alarm	der Alarm	*dayr alarm*
alarm clock	der Wecker	*dayr vekker*
alcohol	der Alkohol	*dayr alkohol*
allergic	allergisch	*allayrgish*
alone	allein	*allain*
always	immer	*immer*
ambulance	der Rettungswagen	*dayr rettoongs vargen*
amount	der Betrag	*dayr betrarg*
amusement park	der Vergnügungspark	*dayr fayr gnue goongs park*
anchovy	die Anschovis	*dee antshoveez*
and	und	*oont*
angry	böse	*boezer*
animal	das Tier	*dass teer*
ankle	der Knöchel	*dayr knoekhel*
answer	die Antwort	*dee antvort*
ant	die Ameise	*dee armaizer*
antibiotics	das Antibiotikum	*dass antee beeotee kum*
antifreeze	das Frostschutzmittel	*dass frost shoots mittel*

antique	alt/(books)	alt/
	antiquarisch	anteekvarish
antiques	die Antiquität	dee antee kveetayt
anus	der After	dayr after
apartment	das Appartement	dass appartamong
aperitif	der Aperitif	dayr appereeteef
apologies	die Entschuldigung	dee ent shooldigoong
apple	der Apfel	dayr apfel
apple juice	der Apfelsaft	dayr apfelzaft
apple pie	der Apfelkuchen	dayr apfel kookhen
apple sauce	das Apfelmus	dass apfel moos
appointment	der Termin	dayr termeen
apricot	die Aprikose	dee apree koazer
	(Aus.) die Marille	dee Mariller
April	der April	dayr aprill
Archbishop	der Erzbischof	dayr airts bishoaf
architecture	die Architektur	dee arkhee tektoor
area	die Umgebung	dee oom gay boong
arena	die Manege	dee manerjer
arm	der Arm	dayr arm
arrange	(sich) verabreden	(sikh) fayr aprayden
arrive	ankommen	ankommen
arrow	der Pfeil	dayr pfail
art	die Kunst	dee koonst
artery	die Schlagader	dee shlarkarder
artichokes	die Artischocke	dee artee shokker
article	der Artikel	dayr arteekel
artificial respiration	die künstliche	dee kuenstlikher
	Beatmung	beart moong
ashtray	der Aschenbecher	dayr ashenbekher
ask	fragen	frargen
ask for	bitten um	bitten oom
asparagus	der Spargel	dayr shpargel
aspirin	das Aspirin	dass asspireen
assault	die Vergewaltigung	dee fayr gevaltee goong
at home	zu Hause	tsoo howzer
at the front	vorn	forn
at the latest	spätestens	shpaytestenz
aubergine	die Aubergine	dee owberjeener
August	der August	dayr owgoost
automatic	automatisch	owtow mar teesh
autumn	der Herbst	dayr hayrpst
avalanche	die Lawine	dee laveener
awake	wach	varkh
awning	das Vordach	dass fordakh

B

baby	das Baby	dass baybee
baby food	die Babynahrung	dee baybee nahroong
babysitter	der Babysitter	dayr baybee zitter
back (at the)	hinten	hinten
back	der Rücken	dayr ruekken
bacon	der Speck	dayr shpek
bad	schlecht/schlimm	shlekht/shlim
bag	die Tasche	dee tasher
bakery	der Bäckerei	dee bekerai
balcony	der Balkon	dayr balkoan

ball	der Ball	*dayr barl*
ballet	das Ballett	*dass balett*
ballpoint pen	der Kugelschreiber/	*dayr koogel shraiber/*
	der Kuli	*dayr koolee*
banana	die Banane	*dee banarner*
bandage	der Verband	*dayr fayrbant*
bank (river)	das Ufer	*dass oofer*
bank	die Bank	*dee bank*
bank pass	die Scheckkarte	*dee shekkarter*
bar	die Bar	*dee bar*
barbecue	das Barbecue	*dass barbekyu*
basketball (to play)	das Baskettballspiel	*dass basket barl shpeel*
bath	das Bad	*dass bart*
bath attendant	der Bademeister	*dayr barder maister*
bath foam	das Schaumbad	*dass showmbart*
bath towel	das Handtuch/(large)	*dass hanttookh/*
	das Badelaken	*dass barder larken*
bathing cap	die Badekappe	*dee barder kapper*
bathing cubicle	die Badekabine	*dee barder kabeener*
bathing suit	der Badeanzug	*dayr barder antsook*
bathroom	das Badezimmer	*dass barder tsimmer*
battery	die Batterie	*dee batteree*
be in love with	verliebt sein in	*fayrleept zain in*
beach	der Strand	*dayr shtrant*
beans	die Bohnen	*dee boanen*
beautiful	schön/prächtig	*shoen/prekhtikh*
beauty parlour	der Kosmetiksalon	*dayr kozmaytik zalong*
bed	das Bett	*dass bett*
bee	die Biene	*dee beener*
beef	das Rindfleisch	*dass rintflaish*
beer	das Bier	*dass beer*
beetroot	die rote Bete	*dee roater bayter*
begin	anfangen/beginnen	*anfangen/beginnen*
beginner	der Anfänger	*dayr anfenger*
behind	(prep.) hinter/	*hinter/*
	(adj.) hinten	*hinten*
Belgian	der Belgier/	*dayr bellgiyer/*
	die Belgierin	*dee bellgiyerin*
Belgium	Belgien	*bellgiyen*
belt	der Gürtel	*dayr guertel*
berth	der Liegeplatz	*dayr leeger plats*
better	besser	*besser*
bicycle	das Fahrrad	*dass far rart*
bicycle pump	die Luftpumpe	*dee looft poomper*
	(fürs Fahrrad)	*(fuers far rart)*
bicycle repairman	der Fahrradhändler	*dayr farrart hendler*
bikini	der Bikini	*dayr bikeeni*
bill	die Rechnung	*dee rekhnoong*
billiards (to play)	Billard spielen	*billyard shpeelen*
birthday	der Geburtstag	*dayr geboorts tark*
biscuit	der Biskuit/der Keks	*dayr biskveet/keks*
bite (to)	beissen	*baissen*
bitter	bitter	*bitter*
black	schwarz	*shvarts*
bland	geschmacklos	*geshmakkloass*
blanket	die Decke	*dee dekker*
bleach	blondieren	*blondeeren*

Word list

15

117

blister	die Blase	dee blarzer
blond	blond	blont
blood	das Blut	dass bloot
blood pressure	der Blutdruck	dayr bloot drook
blouse	die Bluse	dee bloozer
blow dry	föhnen	foenen
blue	blau	blow
board (on)	an Bord	an bort
boat	das Boot	dass boat
body	der Körper	dayr koerper
body milk	die Bodylotion	dee body loa tseeoan
boiled	gekocht	gekokht
bonbon	die Praline/	dee praleener/
	das Bonbon	dass bonbon
bone	der Knochen	dayr knokhen
bonnet	die Motorhaube	dee moator howber
book (to)	reservieren	rezayrveeren
book	das Buch	dass bookh
booked	reserviert	rezayrveert
booking office	die Vorverkaufsstelle	dee for fayrkowfs shteller
bookshop	die Buchhandlung	dee bookh hand loong
border	die Grenze	dee grentser
bored (to be)	sich langweilen	zikh langvailen
boring	langweilig	langvailikh
born	geboren	geboren
borrow	ausleihen	owslaihen
botanical gardens	der Botanische Garten	dayr boatarnisher garten
both	beides	baidez
bottle	die Flasche	dee flasher
bottle-warmer	der Flaschenwärmer	dayr flashen vermer
box	der Karton	dayr karton
box	die Loge	dee loajer
boy	der Junge	dayr yoonger
bra	der BH	dayr bayhar
bracelet	das Armband	dass armbant
braised	gedünstet/gesotten	geduenstet/gezotten
brake	die Bremse	dee bremzer
brake fluid	die Bremsflüssigkeit	dee bremz fluessikh kait
brake oil	das Bremsöl	dass bremzoel
bread	das Brot	dass broat
break	(zer-)brechen	(tsair-)brekhen
breakfast	das Frühstück	dass frueshtuek
breast	die Brust	dee broost
bridge	die Brücke	dee brueker
briefs	der Schlüpfer	dayr shluepfer
bring	(mit-)bringen	(mit-)bringen
brochure	die Broschüre	dee broashuerer
broken	kaputt	kapoott
brother	der Bruder	dayr brooder
brown	braun	brown
brush	die Bürste	dee buerster
Brussels sprouts	der Rosenkohl	dayr rozenkoal
bucket	der Eimer	dayr aimer
bug	das Ungeziefer	dass oon getseefer
building	das Gebäude	dass geboyder

buoy	die Boje	_dee boayer_
burglary	der Einbruch	_dayr ainbrookh_
burn	verbrennen	_fair brennen_
burnt	angebrannt	_angebrant_
bus	der (Auto-)Bus	_dayr (owtoa-) booss_
bus station	der Busbahnhof	_dayr booss barnhoaf_
bus stop	die Bushaltestelle	_dee booss halter shteller_
business class	Business Class	_bizniss klarss_
business trip	die Geschäftsreise	_dee geshefts raizer_
busy	lebhaft/geschäftig	_layphaft/gesheftikh_
butane camping gas	das Butangas	_dass bootarn gass_
butcher	der Schlachter/	_dayr shlakhter/_
	der Metzger	_dayr mettsger_
butter	die Butter	_dee bootter_
button	der Knopf	_dayr knopf_
buy	kaufen	_kowfen_
by airmail	per Luftpost	_payr looftpost_

C

cabbage	der Kohl	_dayr koal_
cabin	die Kabine	_dee kabeener_
cake	der Kuchen/	_dayr kukhen/_
	das (Stück) Gebäck	_dass (shtuek) gebeck_
cake	die Torte	_dee torter_
cake shop	die Konditorei	_dee kondeetorai_
call	anrufen	_anroofen_
called (to be)	heissen	_haissen_
camera	die Kamera	_dee kammerar_
camp	campen	_kampen_
camp shop	der Campingladen	_dayr kamping larden_
camp site	der Campingplatz	_dayr kamping plats_
camper	das Wohnmobil	_dass voan moabeel_
campfire	das Lagerfeuer	_dass larger foyer_
camping guide	der Campingführer	_dayr kamping fuerer_
camping permit	die Camping-	_dee kamping_
	erlaubnis	_ayrlowpniss_
cancel (to)	annullieren	_annooleeren_
candle	die Kerze	_dee kayrtser_
canoe (to)	Kanu fahren	_kanoo faren_
canoe	das Kanu	_dass kanoo_
car	das Auto	_dass owtoa_
car	der Waggon	_dayr vaggorn_
car deck	das Autodeck	_dass owtoa deck_
car documents	die Fahrzeugpapiere	_dee far tsoyk papeerer_
car park (multi-storey)	die Parkgarage	_dee parkgararjer_
car seat	der Kindersitz	_dayr kinderzits_
car trouble	die Panne	_dee panner_
carafe	die Karaffe	_dee karaffer_
caravan	der Wohnwagen	_dayr voan vargen_
cardigan	die Jacke	_dee yakker_
careful	vorsichtig	_forzikhtikh_
carrot	die Karotte	_dee karotter_
carton of cigarettes	die Stange	_dee shtanger_
	Zigaretten	_tsigaretten_
cascade	der Wasserfall	_dayr vasserfall_
cash desk	die Kasse	_dee kasser_

Word list

15

English	German	Pronunciation
casino	das Kasino	*dass kasseeno*
cassette	die Cassette	*dee kassetter*
castle	das Schloss	*dass shloss*
cat	die Katze	*dee kattser*
catalogue	der Katalog	*dayr kataloag*
cathedral	die Kathedrale	*dee kattee drarler*
cauliflower	der Blumenkohl	*dayr bloomen koal*
	(S.Ger.,Aus.) der Karfiol	*dayr karfeeol*
cave	die Höhle	*dee hoehler*
CD	die CD	*dee tsaydee*
celebrate	feiern	*faiern*
cellotape	das Klebeband	*dass klayberbant*
cemetery	der Friedhof	*dayr freethoaf*
centimetre	der/das Zentimeter	*dayr/dass tsen tee mayter*
central heating	die Zentralheizung	*dee tsentrarl hai tsoong*
centre	die Mitte	*dee mitter*
centre	das Zentrum	*dass tsen troom*
chair	der Stuhl	*dayr shtool*
chambermaid	das Zimmermädchen	*dass tsimmer maydkhen*
champagne	der Champagner/Sekt	*dayr shampanyer/zekt*
change (alter)	ändern	*endern*
change (one thing for another)	wechseln	*vekhseln*
change (trains)	umsteigen	*oomshtaigen*
change the baby's nappy	wickeln	*vikkeln*
chapel	die Kapelle	*dee kappeller*
charter flight	der Charterflug	*dayr charter flook*
chat up	jemand anmachen/ sich jemand angeln	*yaymant anmakhen/ zikh yaymant angeln*
check	kontrollieren	*kontrolleeren*
check in	sich anmelden	*zikh anmelden*
cheers	Prost/zum Wohl	*prost/tsoom voal*
cheese (mature, mild)	der Käse (alte, junge)	*dayr kayzer (alter, yoonger)*
chef	der Chef	*dayr shef*
chemist	die Drogerie	*dee drogeree*
cheque	der Scheck	*dayr shek*
cherries	Kirschen	*dee keershen*
chess	das Schachspiel	*dass shakhshpeel*
chewing gum	der/das Kaugummi	*dayr/dass kowgoomee*
chicken	das Huhn/Hühnchen/ Hähnchen	*dass hoon/huenkhen/ haynkhen*
chicory	der Chicorée	*dayr chikoree*
child	das Kind	*dass kint*
child's seat	der Kindersitz	*dayr kinderzits*
chilled	gekühlt	*gekuehlt*
chin	das Kinn	*dass kinn*
chips	Pommes frites	*pomm frits*
chocolate	die Schokolade	*dee shoko larder*
choose	wählen	*vaylen*
chop	das Kotelett	*dass kotlayt*
christian name	der Vorname	*dayr fornarmer*
church	die Kirche	*dee keerkher*

Word list

15

120

church service	der Gottesdienst	dayr gottes deenst
cigar	die Zigarre	dee tseegarrer
cigar shop	der Tabakladen	dayr tarbak larden/
cigarette	die Zigarette	dee tseegaretter
cigarette paper	das Zigarettenpapier	dass tseegaretten papeer
ciné camera	die Filmkamera	dee film kamerar
circle	der Kreis	dayr krais
circus	der Zirkus	dayr tseerkooss
city map	der Stadtplan	dayr shtatplarn
classical concert	das Klassikkonzert	dass klasseek kontsert
clean	saubermachen	zowber makhen
clean	sauber	zowber
clear	deutlich	doytlikh
clearance	der Ausverkauf	dayr owsfairkowf
clock	die Uhr	dee ooer
closed	geschlossen	geshlossen
closed off	gesperrt	geshpayrrt
clothes	die Kleider	dee klaider
clothes hanger	der Kleiderbügel	dayr klaider buegel
clothes peg	die Wäscheklammer	dee vesher klammer
clothing (piece of)	das Kleidungsstück	dass klaidoongs shtook
clothing	die Kleidung	dee klaidoong
coach	der Reisebus	dayr raizerbooss
coat	der Mantel	dayr mantel
cockroach	der Kakerlak	dayr karkerlak
cocoa	der Kakao	dayr kakow
cod	der Kabeljau	dayr karbelyow
coffee	der Kaffee	dayr kaffay
coffee filter	der Kaffeefilter	dayr kaffay filtor
cognac	der Kognak	dayr konyak
cold	kalt	kalt
cold (a)	die Erkältung	dee ayrkeltoong
cold cuts	der Aufschnitt	dayr owfshnit
collarbone	das Schlüsselbein	dass shluessel bain
colleague	der Kollege	dayr kolleger
collision	der Zusammenstoss	dayr tsoo zammen shtoas
cologne	das Eau de toilette	dass oadetwalet
colour	die Farbe	dee farber
colour pencils	die Buntstifte	dee boont shtifter
colour TV	der Farbfernseher	dayr farp fayrn zayer
colouring book	das Malbuch	dass marlbookh
comb	der Kamm	dayr kamm
come	kommen	kommen
come back	zurückkommen	tsooruek kommen
compartment	das Abteil	dass aptail
complaint (physical)	das Leiden	dass laiden
complaint	die Beschwerde/	dee beshverder/
	die Beanstandung	dee bean shtan doong
complaints book	das Beschwerdebuch	dass beshvayrder bookh
completely	ganz	gants
compliment	das Kompliment	dass kompleement
compulsory	verpflichtet	fayrpflikhtet
concert	das Konzert	dass kontsayrt

concert hall	die Konzerthalle	dee kontsayrt haller
concussion	die Gehirn-erschütterung	dee geheern ayr shuete roong
condensed milk	die Kaffeemilch/die Kondensmilch	dee kaffay milkh/dee kondens milkh
condom	das Kondom/der Pariser/das Gummi	dass kondoam/dayr pareeser/dass goommee
congratulate	gratulieren	gratoo leeren
connection	die Verbindung	dee fayr bin doong
constipation	die Verstopfung	dee fayr shtop foong
consulate	das Konsulat	dass konsoolart
consultation	die Konsultation	dee kon sool tat tseeoan
contact lens	die Kontaktlinse	dee kontakt linzer
contact lens solution	das Kontaktlinsen-mittel	dass kontakt linzen mittel
contagious	ansteckend	anshtekent
contraceptive	das Verhütungsmittel	dass fayr hue toongs mittel
contraceptive pill	die Verhütungspille	dee fayr hue toongs piller
cook (verb)	kochen	kokhen
cook	der Koch	dayr kokh
copper	das Kupfer	dass koopfer
copy	die Kopie	dee kopee
corkscrew	der Korkenzieher	dayr korken tseeher
corn flour	das Maizena	dass maitsenar
corner	die Ecke	dee ekker
correct	korrekt	korrekt
correspond	korrespondieren	korrespondeeren
corridor	der Flur	dayr flooer
costume	der Anzug	dayr antsook
cot	das Kinderbett	dass kinderbett
cotton	die Baumwolle	dee bowmvoller
cotton wool	die Watte	dee vatter
cough	der Husten	dayr hoosten
cough mixture	der Hustensaft	dayr hoostenzaft
counter	der Schalter	dayr shalter
country	das Land	dass lant
country code	die Ländernummer	dee lender noommer
courgette	die Zucchini	dee tsookeenee
course	(med.) die Kur	dee koor
cousin	(m)der Cousin/(f)die Cousine	dayr koozeen/dee koozeener
crab	die Krabbe	dee krabber
cream	die Creme	dee kraymer
cream (for cooking)	die Sahne/der Rahm	dee zarner/dayr rarm
credit card	die Kreditkarte	dee kredeet karter
crisps	die Chips	dee chips
croissant	das Croissant/das Hörnchen	dass krwassan/dass hoernshen
cross (the road)	überqueren	ueber kvayren
crossing	die Überfahrt	dee ueberfart
cry	weinen	vainen
cubic metre	der/das Kubikmeter	dayr/dass koobeek mayter

cucumber	die (Salat)gurke	dee (zalart)goorker
cuddly toy	das Kuscheltier	dass kooshelteer
cuff links	die Manschetten knöpfe	dee man shetten knoepfer
cup	die Tasse	dee tasser
	(Aus.) die Schale	dee sharler
curly	lockig	lokikh
current	die Strömung	dee shtroemoong
cushion	das Kissen	dass kissen
customary	üblich	ueblikh
customs	der Zoll/die Zoll-kontrolle	dayr tsoll/dee tsol-kontroller
cut	schneiden	shnaiden
cutlery	das Besteck	dass beshtek
cycle	fahrradfahren	far-rart fahren

D

daily	jeden Tag	yayden tark
dairy products	Molkereiprodukte	molkerai prodookter
damaged	beschädigt	beshaydikt
dance	tanzen	tantsen
danger	die Gefahr	dee gefar
dangerous	gefährlich	gefayrlikh
dark	dunkel	doonkel
date	die Verabredung	dee fayr ap ray doong
daughter	die Tochter	dee tokhter
day	der Tag	dayr tark
day before yesterday	vorgestern	forgestern
dead	tot	toat
decaffeinated	koffeinfrei	koffayeen frai
December	der Dezember	dayr detsember
deck chair	der Strandstuhl/ Strandkorb	dayr shtrantshtool/ dayr shtrantkorp
declare (customs)	verzollen	fayrtsollen
deep	tief	teef
deepfreeze	einfrieren	ainfreeren
degrees	Grad	grart
delay	die Verspätung	dee fayrshpaytoong
delicious	vorzüglich	fortsueglikh
dentist	der Zahnarzt/ der Dentist	dayr tsarnartst/ der denteest
dentures	das Kunstgebiss	dass koonstgebiss
deodorant	das Deo(dorant)	dass deo(dorant)
department	die Abteilung	dee aptailoong
department store	das Kaufhaus	dass kowfhows
departure	die Abfahrt/(flight) der Abflug	dee apfahrt/ dayr apflook
departure time	die Abfahrtszeit	dee apfahrts tsait
depilatory cream	die Enthaarungs creme	dee ent hahroongs kraymer
deposit (to)	zur Aufbewahrung (geben)	tsoor owf bevaroong (gayben)
deposit	die Kaution	dee kowtseeoan
dessert	die Nachspeise	dee nakhshpaizer
destination	das (End)ziel	dass (ent)tseel
destination (mail)	der Bestimmungsort	dayr be shtimoongs ort

Word list

15

develop	entwickeln	*entvikkeln*
diabetic	(m.) der Diabetiker/	*dayr deearbayteeker/*
	(f.) die Diabetikerin	*dee deearbayteekerin*
dial	wählen	*vaylen*
diamond	der Diamant	*dayr deearmant*
diarrhoea	der Durchfall	*dayr doorkhfall*
dictionary	das Wörterbuch	*dass voerter bookh*
diesel	der Diesel	*dayr deezel*
diet	die Diät	*dee deeyayt*
difficulty	die Schwierigkeit	*dee shveerikh kait*
dining room	der Speisesaal	*dayr shpaizerzaal*
dining/buffet car	der Speisewagen	*dayr shpaizer vargen*
dinner (to have)	zu Abend essen	*tsoo arbent essen*
dinner	das Abendessen	*dass arbentessen*
dinner jacket	der Smoking	*dayr smoking*
direction	die Richtung	*dee rikhtoong*
directly	direkt	*deerekt*
dirty	schmierig/schmutzig	*shmeerikh/shmootsikh*
disabled	der/die Behin-	*dayr/dee behin*
	derte	*dayrter*
disco	die Disko	*dee disko*
discount	die Ermässigung/	*dee ermaysi goong/*
	der Nachlass	*dayr nakhlass*
dish	das Gericht	*dass gerikht*
dish of the day	das Tagesgericht	*dass targes gerikht*
disinfectant	das Desinfektions-	*dass dez infektseey*
	mittel	*oanzmittel*
distance	die Entfernung	*dee entfayr noong*
distilled water	das destillierte	*dass destileerter*
	Wasser	*vasser*
disturb	stören	*shtoeren*
disturbance	die Störung	*dee shtoeroong*
dive	tauchen	*towkhen*
diving	der Tauchsport	*dayr towkhshport*
diving (deep sea)	das Tiefseetauchen	*dass teefzaytowkhen*
diving board	das Sprungbrett	*dass shproongbret*
diving gear	die Taucher-	*dee towkher*
	ausrüstung	*owsruestoong*
divorced	geschieden	*gesheeden*
DIY-shop	der Heimwerkermarkt	*dayr haim vayrker markt*
dizzy	schwind(e)lig	*shvind(e)likh*
do	tun	*toon*
doctor	der Arzt/(lady)	*dayr artst/*
	die Ärztin	*dee ayrtstin*
dog	der Hund	*dayr hoont*
doll	die Puppe	*dee pupper*
domestic	das Inland	*dass inlant*
done (cooked)	gar	*gar*
door	die Tür	*dee tuer*
double	Doppel-	*doppel-*
down	unten	*oonten*
draught	der Zug	*dayr tsook*
draughts	das Damespiel	*dass darmeshpeel*
dream	träumen	*troymen*
dress	das Kleid	*dass klait*
dressing gown	der Morgenmantel	*dayr morgen mantel*
drink	trinken	*trinken*

Word list

15

drinking water	das Trinkwasser	dass trinkvasser
drive	fahren	faren
driver	der Fahrer	dayr farer
driving licence	der Führerschein	dayr fuerershain
drought	die Trockenheit	dee trokkenhait
dry	trocknen	trokknen
dry	trocken	trokken
dry clean	reinigen	rainigen
dry cleaner's	die Reinigung	dee rainigoong
dry shampoo	das Pudershampoo/	dass pooder shampoo/
	das Trockenshampoo	dass trokken shampoo
dummy	der Schnuller	dayr shnooller
during	während	vayrent
during the day	tagsüber	targsueber

E

ear	das Ohr	dass oa-er
ear, nose and throat (ENT) specialist	der Hals-, Nasen-Ohrenarzt (HNO)	dayr halz-, narzen-, oarenartst (har enn oh)
earache	die Ohrenschmerzen	dee oarenshmairtsen
eardrops	die Ohrentropfen	dee oarentropfen
early	früh	frueh
earrings	die Ohrringe	dee oarringer
earth	die Erde	dee erder
earthenware	die Keramik	dee kayrarmik
east	der Osten	dayr osten
easy	leicht/(comfortable)	laikht/
	bequem	bekvaym
eat	essen	essen
eczema	das Ekzem	dass ektsaym
eel	der Aal	dayr arl
egg	das Ei	dass ai
elastic band	das Gummi	dass goomee
electric	elektrisch	elektrish
electricity	der Strom	dayr shtroam
embassy	die Botschaft	dee boatshaft
emergency brake	die Notbremse	dee noat bremzer
emergency exit	der Notausgang	dayr noat owsgang
emergency number	die Notrufnummer	dee noat roof noommer
emergency phone	die Notrufsäule	dee noat roof zoyler
emery board	die Nagelfeile	dee nargelfailer
empty	leer	layr
engaged (to be married)	verlobt	fayrloabt
engaged	besetzt	bezetst
England	England	englant
English	englisch	english
Englishman	der Engländer	dayr englender
Englishwoman	die Engländerin	dee englenderin
enjoy	genießen	geneessen
entertainment guide	der Veranstaltungs-kalender	dayr fayr anshtal toongs kalender
envelope	der Umschlag	dayr umshlark
escort	die Begleitung	dee beglaitoong
evening	der Abend	dayr arbent
evening wear	die Abendkleidung	dee arbent klai doong
event	die Veranstaltung	dee fair an shtal toong
every time	jedesmal	yaydezmarl

Word list

15

125

everything	alles	*alless*
everywhere	überall	*ueberarl*
examine	untersuchen	*oonter zookhen*
excavation	die Ausgrabung	*dee owsgraaboong*
excellent	ausgezeichnet	*ows getsaikh net*
exchange	(aus)tauschen	*(ows)towshen*
exchange office	das Wechselbüro	*dass vekhsel buero*
exchange rate	der Wechselkurs	*dayr vekhselkoors*
excursion	der Ausflug	*dayr owsflook*
exhibition	die Ausstellung	*dee owsshteloong*
exit	der Ausgang	*dayr owsgang*
expenses	die Unkosten	*dee oonkosten*
expensive	teuer	*toyer*
explain	erklären	*ayrklayren*
express	der Schnellzug	*dayr shnelltsoog*
external	äusserlich	*oysserlikh*
eye	das Auge	*dass owger*
eyedrops	die Augentropfen	*dee owgentropfen*
eyeshadow	der Lidschatten	*dayr leetshatten*
eye specialist	der Augenarzt	*dayr owgenartst*
eyeliner	der Eyeliner	*dayr ailainer*

F

face	das Gesicht	*dass gezikht*
factory	die Fabrik	*dee fabreek*
fair	die Kirmes	*dee keermess*
fall	stürzen/fallen	*shtuertsen/fallen*
family	die Familie	*dee fameelier*
famous	berühmt	*beruemt*
far away	weit weg	*vait vek*
farm	der Bauernhof	*dayr bowernhoaf*
farmer	der Bauer	*dayr bower*
farmer's wife	die Bäuerin	*dee boyerin*
fashion	die Mode	*dee moader*
fast	schnell	*shnell*
father	der Vater	*dayr farter*
fault	die Schuld	*dee shoolt*
fax	telefaxen	*teleefaksen*
February	der Februar	*dayr febrooar*
	(Aus.) der Feber	*dayr fayber*
feel	fühlen	*fuelen*
feel like	Lust haben	*loost harben*
fence	der Zaun	*dayr tsown*
ferry	die Fähre	*dee fayrer*
fever	das Fieber	*dass feeber*
fill	füllen	*fuelen*
fill out	ausfüllen	*owsfuellen*
filling	die Füllung	*dee fuelloong*
film	der Film	*dayr film*
filter	der/das Filter	*dayr/dass filter*
find	finden	*finden*
fine	der Strafzettel	*dayr shtrarftsettel*
finger	der Finger	*dayr finger*
fire	das Feuer	*das foyer*
fire brigade	die Feuerwehr	*dee foyer vayr*
fire escape	die Feuertreppe	*dee foyer trepper*
fire extinguisher	der Feuerlöscher	*dayr foyer loesher*

Word list

15

first	erst/erste/erster	*ayrst/ayrster/ayrster*
first aid	die Erste Hilfe	*dee ayrster hilfer*
first class	erster Klasse	*ayrster klasser*
fish (verb)	angeln	*angeln*
fish	der Fisch	*dayr fish*
fishing rod	die Angel	*dee angel*
fit	passen	*passen*
fitness centre	das Fitness-Zentrum	*dass fitness-tsentroom*
fitness training	das Fitness-Training	*dass fitness-trayneeng*
fitting room	die Anprobekabine	*dee an prober kabeener*
fix	flicken	*flikken*
flag	die Fahne/die Flagge	*dee farner/dee flagger*
flash bulb	das Blitzbirnchen	*dass blitz birn khen*
flash cube	der Blitzwürfel	*dayr blitzvuerfel*
flash gun	das Blitzgerät	*dass blitzgerayt*
flat	die Etagenwohnung	*dee etarjen voh noong*
flea market	der Flohmarkt	*dayr flohmarkt*
flight	der Flug	*dayr flook*
flight number	die Flugnummer	*dee flooknoommer*
flood	die Überschwem- mung	*dee ueber shwem moong*
floor	der Stock/die Etage	*dayr shtok/dee etarjer*
flounder	die Flunder	*dee floonder*
flour	das Mehl	*dass mayhl*
flu	die Grippe	*dee gripper*
fly (insect)	die Fliege	*dee fleeger*
fly (verb)	fliegen	*fleegen*
fly-over	das Viadukt	*dass fiadookt*
fog	der Nebel	*dayr naybel*
foggy (to be)	neblig sein	*nayblikh zain*
folding caravan	der Faltwagen	*dayr faltvargen*
folkloristic	folkloristisch	*folkloristish*
follow	folgen	*folgen*
food	Lebensmittel	*laybens mittel*
food poisoning	die Lebensmittel- vergiftung	*dee laybenzmittel fairgif toong*
foot	der Fuss	*dayr fooss*
for	vor	*for*
forbidden	verboten	*fairboaten*
forehead	die Stirn	*dee shtirn*
foreign	ausländisch	*owslendish*
forget	vergessen	*fairgessen*
fork	die Gabel	*dee garbel*
form	das Formular	*dass formoolar*
fort	die Festung	*dee festoong*
forward	nachschicken	*nakhshikken*
fountain	der Springbrunnen	*dayr shpring broonnen*
frame	das Gestell	*dass geshtel*
franc	der Franken	*dayr franken*
free	frei	*frai*
free	gratis	*grartis*
free time	die Freizeit	*dee fraitsait*
freeze	gefrieren	*gefreeyeren*
French	französisch	*frantsoezish*
French bread	das Stangenweiss brot/die Baguette	*dass shtangenvaiss broat/dee baguetter*

fresh	frisch	*frish*
Friday	der Freitag	*dayr fraitark*
fried	gebacken	*gebacken*
fried egg	das Spiegelei	*dass shpeegelai*
friend	der Freund	*dayr froynt*
friendly	freundlich	*froyntlikh*
frightened	ängstlich	*enkstlikh*
fruit	das Obst	*dass oapst*
fruit juice	der Obstsaft	*dayr oapstzaft*
frying pan	die (Brat)pfanne	*dee (brart)pfanner*
full	voll	*foll*
fun	das Vergnügen/	*dass fergnuegen/*
	der Spass	*dayr shpass*

G

gallery	die Galerie	*dee galleree-er*
game	das Spiel(chen)	*dass shpeel(khen)*
garage	die Werkstatt	*dee verkshtatt*
garbage bag	der Müllsack	*dayr muelzak*
garden	der Garten	*dayr garten*
gas (propane camping)	das Campinggas	*dass kamping gas*
	(das Propangas)	*(dass proaparn gas)*
gastroenteritis	die Magen- und	*dee margen- oont*
	Darmbeschwerden	*darmbeshvayrden*
gate	das Tor	*dass torr*
gauze	der Verbandmull	*dayr fayrbantmool*
gear	der Gang	*dayr gang*
gel	das Gel	*dass jel*
German	deutsch	*doytsh*
Germany	Deutschland	*doytshlant*
get lost	sich verirren	*zikh fayreeren*
get married	heiraten	*hai-rarten*
get off	aussteigen	*owsshtaigen*
gift	das Geschenk	*dass geshenk*
gilt	vergoldet	*fairgoldet*
ginger	der Ingwer	*dayr ingver*
girl	das Mädchen	*dass maydkhen*
girlfriend	die Freundin	*dee froyndin*
giro cheque	der Postbarscheck	*dayr posst barshek*
giro pass	die Giroscheckkarte	*dee geero shek karter*
glacier	der Gletscher	*dayr gletsher*
glass	das Glas	*dass glas*
glasses (sun)	die Sonnenbrille	*dee zonnen briller*
gliding	das Segelfliegen	*dass zaygel fleegen*
glove	der Handschuh	*dayr hantshoo*
glue	der Klebstoff	*dayr klaypshtoff*
gnat	die Mücke	*dee muekker*
go (on foot)	gehen	*gayhen*
go back	zurückgehen/(car)	*tsueruek gayhen/*
	zurückfahren	*tsueruek faren*
go out	ausgehen	*owsgayhen*
goat's cheese	der Ziegenkäse	*dayr tseegen kayzer*
gold	das Gold	*dass golt*
golf	das Golfspiel	*dass golfshpeel*
golf course	der Golfplatz	*dayr golfplats*
gone	weg	*vek*

good day	guten Tag	gooten tark
	(Aus. servus)	zairvoos
	(Sw. Grüezi)	gruetsee
good evening	guten Abend	gooten arbent
good morning	guten Morgen	gooten morgen
good night	gute Nacht	gooter nakht
goodbye	der Abschied	dayr apsheet
gram	das Gramm	dass gramm
grandchild	das Enkelkind	dass enkelkint
grandfather	der Opa	dayr oapa
grandmother	die Oma	dee oamar
grape juice	der Traubensaft	dayr trowbenzaft
grapefruit	die Pampelmuse	dee pampel moozer
grapes	die (Wein)trauben	dee (vain)trowben
grave	das Grab	dass grarp
grease	das Fett	dass fett
green	grün	gruen
green card	die grüne Karte	dee gruener karter
greet	begrüssen	begruessen
grey	grau	grow
grill	grillen	grillen
grilled	geröstet	geroestet
grocer	der Kaufmann/	dayr kowfmann/
	Gemüsehändler	gemueser haentler
ground	der Boden	dayr boaden
group	die Gruppe	dee grupper
guest house	die Pension	dee penseeoan
guide (person/book)	der Führer	dayr fuehrer
guided tour	die Führung	dee fueroong
gynaecologist	der Frauenarzt	dayr frowenartst

H

hair	das Haar	dass har
hairbrush	die Haarbürste	dee harbuerster
hairdresser	der Damen-, Herren-	dayr darmen-, hayrren
	frisör	frizoer
hairpins	die Haarnadeln/	dee harnardeln/
	Haarklemmen	harklemmen
hairspray	das Haarspray	dass harspray
half	halb	halp
half	die Hälfte	dee helfter
half full	halb voll	halp foll
ham (boiled)	der Kochschinken	dayr kokhshinken
ham (smoked)	der Räucherschinken	dayr roykher shinken
hammer	der Hammer	dayr hammer
hand	die Hand	dee hant
handbrake	die Handbremse	dee hantbremzer
handbag	die Handtasche	dee hant-tasher
handkerchief	das Taschentuch	dass tashentookh
handmade	handgearbeitet	hant ge ar bai tet
happy	froh	fro
harbour	der Hafen	dayr harfen
hard	hart	hart
hat	der Hut	dayr hoot
hat	die Mütze	dee muetser
hayfever	der Heuschnupfen	dayr hoyshnoopfen
hazelnut	die Haselnuss	dee harzelnooss

head	der Kopf	dayr kopf
headache	die Kopfschmerzen	dee kopf shmer tsen
health	die Gesundheit	dee gezoonthait
health food shop	das Reformgeschäft	dass reform gesheft
hear	hören	hoeren
hearing aid	das Hörgerät	dass hoergerayt
heart	das Herz	dass hayrts
heart patient	der Herzkranke	dayr hayrts kranker
heater	die Heizung	dee haitsoong
heavy	schwer	shvayr
heel	die Ferse	dee fayrzer
heel (shoe)	der Absatz	dayr apzats
hello	Hallo	hullo
helmet	der Helm	dayr helm
help	helfen	helfen
help	die Hilfe	dee hilfer
helping	die Portion	dee portseeyoan
herbal tea	der Kräutertee	dayr kroytertay
herbs	die Gewürze/(green) die Kräuter	dee gevuertser/ dee kroyter
here	hier	heer
here you are	(giving sb sth) hier/ (on finding sb) da bist du ja!/(on finding sth) da ist es ja!	heer/dar bist doo yar/ dar ist ez yar
herring	der Hering	dayr hayring
high	hoch	hokh
high tide	die Flut	dee floot
highchair	der Kinderstuhl	dayr kindershtool
hiking	der Wandersport	dayr vandershport
hiking trip	die Wanderung	dee vanderoong
hip	die Hüfte	dee huefter
hire (for)	zu vermieten	tsoo fairmeeten
hire	mieten	meeten
hitchhike	per Anhalter fahren/ trampen	payr anhalter faren/ trampen
hobby	das Hobby	dass hobby
holiday	der Feiertag	dayr fayertark
holiday	die Ferien/der Urlaub	dee fayreeyen/dayr oorlowp
holiday house	die Ferienwohnung	dee fayreeyen voanoong
holiday park	der Bungalowpark	der bungaloapark
homesickness	das Heimweh	dass haimvay
honest	ehrlich	ayrlikh
honey	der Honig	dayr hoanikh
horizontal	horizontal	horeetsontarl
horrible	scheusslich	shoyslikh
horse	das Pferd	dass pfayrt
hospital	das Krankenhaus (Aus.,Sw.) das Hospital/Spital	dass krankenhowz dass hospitarl dass shpitarl
hospitality	die Gastfreundschaft	dee gast froynt shaft
hot (spicy)	pikant	peekant
hot-water bottle	die Warmflasche	dee vayrm flasher
hotel	das Hotel	dass hotel
hour	die Stunde	dee shtoonder
house	das Haus	dass howz

household items	die Haushaltsartikel	*dee howz halts artee kel*
Houses of Parliament	das Parlaments-gebäude	*dass parlaments geboyder*
housewife	die Hausfrau	*dee hows frow*
how far?	wie weit?	*vee vait?*
how long?	wie lange?	*vee langer?*
how much?	wieviel?	*veefeel?*
how?	wie?	*vee?*
hungry (to be)	hungrig	*hoongrikh*
hurricane	der Orkan	*dayr orkarn*
hurry	die Eile	*dee ailer*
husband	der (Ehe) mann	*dayr (ayher) man*
hut (mountain)	die Berghütte	*dee bairghuetter*
hut	die Hütte	*dee huetter*
hyperventilation	die Hyperventilation	*dee hueper ventee la tseeoan*

I

ice cubes	die Eiswürfel	*dee aiz vuer fell*
ice skating	das Schlittschuh-laufen	*dass shlit shoo lowfen*
icecream	das (Speise)eis	*dass shpaizeraiz*
idea	die Idee	*dee eeday*
identification	der Ausweis	*dayr owsvaiss*
identify	identifizieren	*eedentee fi tsee ren*
ill	krank	*krank*
illness	die Krankheit	*dee krankhait*
imagination	die Vorstellung	*dee forshtelloong*
immediately	sofort	*zofort*
import duty	Einfuhrzölle	*ainfoor tsoeller*
impossible	unmöglich	*oonmoeglikh*
in	in	*in*
in the evening	abends	*arbents*
in the morning	morgens	*morgens*
included	enthalten/einschliesslich	*enthalten/ainshleesslikh*
indicate	zeigen	*tsaigen*
indicator	der Blinker	*dayr blinker*
industrial art	das Kunstgewerbe	*dass koonstgewayrber*
inexpensive	billig	*billikh*
infection (viral, bacterial)	die Virusinfektion, die bakterielle Infektion	*dee veeroos infekts eeoan, dee bakteereey eller infektseeoan*
inflammation	die Entzündung	*dee ent tsuen doong*
information	die Angaben	*dee angarben*
information	die Auskunft	*dee owskunft*
information office	das Auskunftsbüro	*dass ows kunfts bueroh*
injection	die Spritze	*dee shpritser*
injured	verletzt	*fayrletst*
innocent	unschuldig	*oonshooldikh*
insect	das Insekt	*dass inzekt*
insect bite	der Insektenstich	*dayr inzekten shtikh*
insect repellent	das Mückenöl	*dass muekkenoel*
inside	drin(nen)	*drin(nen)*
insole	die Einlegesohle	*dee ainlaygesohler*

instructions	die Gebrauchs-anweisung	dee gebrowkhs anvai zoong
insurance	die Versicherung	dee fayrzikheroong
intermission	die Pause	dee powzer
international	international	eenter natseeoa narl
interpreter	der Dolmetscher	dayr dolmetsher
intersection	die Kreuzung	dee kroytsoong
introduce oneself	sich vorstellen	sikh forshtellen
invite	einladen	ainlarden
iodine	das Jod	dass yot
Ireland	Irland	eerlant
Irish	irländisch	eerlendish
Irishman	der Ire	dayr eerer
Irishwoman	die Irin	dee eerin
iron (verb)	bügeln	byoogelln
iron	das Bügeleisen	dass buegell aizen
ironing board	das Bügelbrett	dass buegelbrett
island	die Insel	dee inzel
Italian	italienisch	italeeaynish
Italy	Italien	itarlee-en
itch	das Jucken	dass yooken

J

jack	der Wagenheber	dayr vargen hayber
jacket	die Jacke	dee yakker
jam	die Marmelade	dee marmelarder
January	der Januar	dayr yanooar/
	(Aus.) der Jenner	dayr yenner
jaw	der Kiefer	dayr keefer
jellyfish	die Qualle	dee kvaller
jeweller	der Juwelier	dayr yoovayleer
jewellery	der Schmuck	dayr shmook
jog	joggen	joggen
joke	der Witz	dayr vits
juice	der Saft	dayr zaft
July	der Juli	dayr yoolee
jumble sale	der Flohmarkt	dayr flohmarkt
jump leads	das Startkabel	dass shtartkarbel
jumper	der Pullover	dayr pullover
June	der Juni	dayr yooni

K

key (ignition)	der Zündschlüssel	dayr tsuent shluessel
key	der Schlüssel	dayr shluessel
kilo	das Kilo	dass keelo
kilometre	der Kilometer	dayr keelo mayter
king	der König	dayr koenikh
kiss (verb)	küssen	kuessen
kiss	der Kuss	dayr kooss
kitchen	die Küche	dee kuekher
knee	das Knie	dass knee
knee socks	Kniestrümpfe	dee knee shtruempfer
knife	das Messer	dass messer
knit	stricken	shtrikken
know	wissen	vissen

L

lace	der Schnürsenkel	*dayr shnuerzenkel*
ladies toilet	die Damentoilette	*dee darmen twalet ter*
lake	der See	*dayr zay*
lamp	die Lampe	*dee lamper*
land	landen	*landen*
lane	die Fahrspur	*dee fahrshpoor*
language	die Sprache	*dee shprakher*
large	gross	*groass*
last	letzte	*letster*
late	spät	*shpayt*
later	nachher	*nakh her*
laugh	lachen	*lakhen*
launderette	die Münzwäscherei	*dee muents vesheray*
law	das Recht	*dass rekht*
laxative	das Abführmittel	*dass ap fuer mittel*
leaded	das Super(benzin)	*dass zooper(bentseen)*
leak	das Loch	*dass lokh*
leather	das Leder	*dass layder*
leather goods	Lederwaren	*layder varen*
leave	abfahren/abfliegen	*apfahren/apfleegen*
leek	der Porree/der Lauch	*dayr porray/dayr lowkh*
left	links	*links*
left	nach links	*nakh links*
leg	das Bein	*dass bain*
lemon	die Zitrone	*dee tsitroner*
lend	leihen	*laihen*
lens (wide-angle)	das Weitwinkel-objektiv	*dass vait vinkel obyek teef*
lens	die Linse	*dee linzer*
lentils	die Linsen	*dee linzen*
less	weniger	*vayniger*
lesson	die Stunde	*dee shtoonder*
letter	der Brief	*dayr breef*
lettuce	der Kopfsalat	*dayr kopfzalart*
level crossing	der Bahnübergang	*dayr barn ueber gang*
library	die Bibliothek	*dee beebleeotayk*
lie (tell lie)	lügen	*luegen*
lie	liegen	*leegen*
lift (hitchhike)	die Mitfahr-gelegenheit	*dee mit far-gelaygenhait*
lift (in building)	der Fahrstuhl/der Aufzug	*dayr farshtool/der owftsook*
lift (ski)	der (Sessel)lift	*dayr (zessel)lift*
light (not dark)	hell	*hell*
light (not heavy)	leicht	*laikht*
lighter	das Feuerzeug	*dass foyer tsoyk*
lighthouse	der Leuchtturm	*dayr loykht toorm*
lightning	der Blitz	*dayr blits*
like	mögen/(stronger) lieben	*moergen/leeben*
line	die Linie	*dee leenier*
linen	das Leinen	*dass lainen*
lipstick	der Lippenstift	*dayr lippen shtift*
liqueur	der Likör	*dayr leekoer*
liquorice	die Lakritze(n)	*dee lakritzer(n)*
listen	(zu)hören	*(tsoo)hoeren*

Word list

15

literature	die Literatur	*dee literatoor*
litre	der/das Liter	*dayr/dass leeter*
little	wenig	*vaynikh*
little (a)	das bisschen, ein bisschen	*dass bis-shen, ain bis-shen*
live	wohnen	*voanen*
live together	zusammenleben	*tsoo zammen layben*
lobster	der Hummer	*dayr hoommer*
local	örtlich	*oertlikh*
lock	das Schloss	*dass shloss*
locker (luggage)	das Schliessfach (für Gepäck)	*dass shleesfakh (fuer gepek)*
long	lang	*lang*
look	schauen	*showern*
look for	suchen	*zookhen*
look up	aufsuchen	*owfzookhen*
lorry	der LKW/der Last-wagen	*dayr ellkarvay/ dayr lasstvargen*
lose	verlieren	*fayrleeren*
loss	der Verlust	*dayr fayrloost*
lost	(gen.)weg/(also people) vermisst	*vek/fayrmisst*
lost	verloren	*fayrloren*
lost property office	das Fundbüro	*dass foontbuero*
lotion	die Lotion	*dee loatseeoan*
loud	laut	*lowt*
love	sich lieben	*zikh leeben*
love	die Liebe	*dee leeber*
low	niedrig	*needrikh*
low tide	die Ebbe	*dee ebber*
luck	das Glück	*dass gluek*
luggage (left)	die Gepäck-aufbewahrung	*dee gepek owfbevaroong*
luggage	das Gepäck	*dass gepek*
luggage locker	das Schliessfach	*dass shleesfakh*
lumps (sugar)	die Zuckerwürfel	*dee tsooker wuerfel*
lunch	das Mittagessen	*dass mittark essen*
lungs	die Lungen	*dee loongen*

M

macaroni	Makkaroni	*makaroanee*
machine (vending)	der Automat	*dayr owtomart*
madam	meine Dame	*mainer darmer*
magazine	die Zeitschrift	*dee tsaitshrift*
mail	die Post	*dee post*
make an appointment	einen Termin machen	*ainen tairmeen makhen*
makeshift	provisorisch	*proveezorish*
manager	der Verwalter	*dayr fayrvalter*
mandarin	die Mandarine	*dee mandareener*
manicure	die Maniküre	*dee manee kuerer*
map	die (Land)karte	*dee (lant)karter*
marble	der Marmor	*dayr marmor*
March	der März	*dayr mayrts*
margarine	die Margarine	*dee margareener*
marina	der Yachthafen	*dayr yakht harfen*
market	der Markt	*dayr markt*

marriage	die Ehe	dee ayher
married	verheiratet	fayrhai-rartet
mass	die Messe	dee messer
massage	die Massage	dee massarjer
match	der Wettkampf	dayr vetkampf
matches	die Streichhölzer	dee shtraikh hoeltser
May	der Mai	dayr mai
maybe	vielleicht	feelaikht
mayonnaise	die Mayonnaise	dee mayonnayzer
mayor	der Bürgermeister	dayr buerger maister
meal	die Mahlzeit	dee marltsait
mean	bedeuten	bedoyten
meat	das Fleisch	dass flaish
medication	das Heilmittel	dass hailmittel
medicine	das Medikament	dass medee kar ment
meet	kennenlernen	kennen layrnen
melon	die Melone	dee melowner
membership	die Mitgliedschaft	dee mitt gleet shaft
menstruate	(meine/ihre) Tage haben	(mainer/eerer) targer harben
menstruation	die Periode	dee peereeoader
menu	das Menü	dass menue
menu	die Speisekarte	dee shpaizer karter
menu of the day	das Tagesmenü	dass targez menue
message	der Bescheid/die Nachricht	dayr beshait/dee nakhrikht
metal	das Metall	dass mettarl
meter	der/das Taxameter	dayr/dass taksamayter
metre	der/das Meter	dayr/dass mayter
migraine	die Migräne	dee meegrayner
mild (tobacco)	(der) leicht(e) (Tabak)	(dayr) laikht(er) (tarbak)
milk	die Milch	dee milkh
millimetre	der/das Millimeter	dayr/dass millimayter
milometer	der Kilometerzahler	dayr keelo mayter tsayler
mince	das Mett/das Hackfleisch	dass met/ dass hackflaish
mineral water	das Mineralwasser	dass minerarl vasser
minute	die Minute	dee meenooter
mirror	der Spiegel	dayr shpeegell
miss	vermissen	fayrmissen
missing (to be)	fehlen	faylen
missing person	vermisste Person	fayrmisster payrzoan
mistake	der Fehler/der Irrtum	dayr fayler/dayr eertoom
mistaken (to be)	sich irren	zikh irren
misunderstanding	das Missverständnis	dass miss fayr shtant nis
mocha	der Mokka	dayr mokker
modern art	die moderne Kunst	dee moderner koonst
molar	der Backenzahn	dayr bakkentsarn
moment	der Augenblick	dayr owgenblik
moment	der Moment	dayr moament
monastery	das Kloster	dass kloaster
Monday	der Montag	dayr moantark
money	das Geld	dass gelt
month	der Monat	dayr moanart
moped	das Moped	dass moaped
mosque	die Moschee	dee moshay

motel	das Motel	*dass moatell*
mother	die Mutter	*dee mooter*
moto-cross	das Moto-Cross	*dass moto-kross*
motorbike	das Motorrad	*dass moatorrart*
motorboat	das Motorboot	*dass moatorboat*
motorway	die Autobahn	*dee owtobarn*
mountain	der Berg	*dayr bayrk*
mountaineering	der Bergsport	*dayr bayrk shporrt*
mouse	die Maus	*dee mows*
mouth	der Mund	*dayr munt*
much/many	viel	*feel*
muscle	der Muskel	*dayr mooskel*
muscle spasms	die Muskelkrämpfe	*dee mooskel krempfer*
museum	das Museum	*dass moozayoom*
mushrooms	die Pilze	*dee piltser*
music	die Musik	*dee moozeek*
musical	das Musical	*dass moozeekall*
mussels	die Muscheln	*dee moosheln*
mustard	der Senf/der Mostrich	*dayr zenf/dayr mosstrikh*

N

nail	der Nagel	*dayr nargel*
nail polish	der Nagellack	*dayr nargellack*
nail polish remover	der Nagellack-entferner	*nargel lack entfair ner*
nail scissors	die Nagelschere	*dee nargelsheerer*
naked	nackt	*nakt*
nappy	die Windel	*dee vindel*
National Health Service	die Krankenkasse	*dee kranken kasser*
nationality	die Staatsangehörig-keit	*dee shtarts an gehoerig kait*
natural	natürlich	*natuerlikh*
nature	die Natur	*dee natoor*
naturism	die Freikörperkultur	*dee fray koerper kooltoor*
nauseous	übel	*uebel*
near	bei	*bai*
nearby	in der Nähe	*in dayr nayher*
necessary	nötig/notwendig	*noetikh/noatvendikh*
neck	der Nacken	*dayr nakken*
necklace	die Kette	*dee ketter*
nectarine	die Nektarine	*dee nektareener*
needle	die Nadel	*dee nardel*
negative	das Negativ	*dass negateef*
neighbours	die Nachbarn	*dee nakhbarn*
nephew	der Neffe	*dayr neffer*
never	nie	*nee*
new	neu	*noy*
news	die Nachricht	*dee nakhrikht*
news-stand	der Kiosk	*dayr keeosk*
newspaper	die Zeitung	*dee tsaitoong*
next	nächste(r)	*nekhste(r)*
next to	neben	*nayben*
nice (friendly)/nice (to the eye)	nett/hübsch	*nett/huepsh*
nice (cosy)	gemütlich	*gemuetlikh*

nice (delicious)	lecker	*lekker*
niece	die Nichte	*dee nikhter*
night	die Nacht	*dee nakht*
night (at)	nachts	*nakhts*
night duty	der Nachtdienst	*dayr nakhtdeenst*
nightclub	der Nachtklub	*dayr nakhtkloop*
nightlife	das Nachtleben	*dass nakhtlayben*
no	nein	*nain*
no overtaking	das Überholverbot	*dass ueber hoal fayr boat*
noise	der Lärm	*dayr layrm*
nonstop	nonstop	*nonstop*
no-one	niemand/keiner	*neemant/kainer*
normal	gewöhnlich	*gevoehnlikh*
north	der Norden	*der norden*
normal	normal	*normarl*
north	nördlich	*noerdlikh*
nose	die Nase	*dee narzer*
nose drops	Nasentropfen	*narzen tropfen*
nosebleed	das Nasenbluten	*dass narzen blooten*
notepaper	das Briefpapier	*dass breefpapeer*
nothing	nichts	*nikhts*
November	der November	*dayr november*
nowhere	nirgendwo	*neergentvo*
nude beach	der Nackt(bade)strand	*dayr nakt(barderr) shtrant*
number	die Nummer	*dee noommer*
number (subscriber's)	die Rufnummer	*dee roof noommer*
number plate	das Nummernschild	*dass noommern shilt*
nurse	die (Kranken)-schwester	*dee (kranken)shvester*
nutmeg	die Muskatnuss	*dee mooskartnooss*
nuts	die Nüsse	*dee nuesser*

O

October	der Oktober	*dayr oktoaber*
off (food)	verdorben	*fairdorben*
offer	anbieten	*anbeeten*
office	das Büro	*dass buero*
off-licence	der Spirituosen-händler	*dayr shpiri too oazen hendler*
oil (diesel)	das Dieselöl	*dass deezeloel*
oil	das Öl	*dass oel*
oil change	der Ölwechsel	*dayr oelvekhsel*
oil level	der Ölstand	*dayr oelshtant*
ointment	die Salbe	*dee zalber*
okay	einverstanden	*ain fayr shtanden*
old	alt	*alt*
olive oil	das Olivenöl	*dass oleevenoel*
olives	die Oliven	*dee oleeven*
omelette	das Omelett	*dass ommlett*
on	auf	*owf*
on the right	rechts	*rekhts*
on the way	unterwegs	*oontervaygs*
oncoming traffic	der Gegenverkehr	*dayr gaygen fayrkayr*
one hundred grams	hundert Gramm	*hoondert gramm*
one-way-traffic	der Einbahnverkehr	*dayr ain barn fayrkayr*
onion	die Zwiebel	*dee tsveebel*

open	öffnen	oeffnen
open	offen	offen
opera	die Oper	dee oaper
operate	operieren	opereeren
operator (telephone)	(m) der Telefonist/(f)	der telefoanist/
	die Telefonistin	dee telefoanistin
operetta	die Operette	dee operetter
opposite	gegenüber	gaygenueber
optician	der Optiker	dayr optiker
or	oder	oader
orange	die Apfelsine/die	dee apfel zeener/
	Orange	dee oranje
orange juice	der Orangensaft	dayr oranjenzaft
order	die Bestellung	dee beshtelloong
order (in), tidy	in Ordnung	in ordnoong
order	bestellen	beshtellen
other	andere/-s	anderer/-s
other side	die andere Seite	dee anderer zaiter
outside	(dr)aussen/(out	(dr)owssen, rows
	wards) raus	
overtake	(overtake) überholen/	ueber hoalen/
	(come alongside)	
	einholen	ainhoalen
oysters	die Austern	dee owstern

P

packed lunch	das Lunchpaket	dass loonch pakayt
pad (writing)	der Schreibblock	dayr shraipblok
	(squared, lined)	
page	die Seite	dee zaiter
pain	der Schmerz,	dayr shmayrts,
	(pl.) Schmerzen	shmayrtsen
painkiller	das Schmerzmittel	dass shmayrts
		mittel
paint	die Farbe	dee farber
painting (art)	die Malerei	dee marlerai
painting (object)	das Gemälde	dass gemelder
palace	der Palast	dayr palast
pan	derTopf	dayr topf
pancake	der Eierkuchen/	dayr aierkookhen/
	der Pfannkuchen	dayr pfann
		kookhen
pane	die Scheibe	dee shayber
panties	der Slip	dayr slip
pants	die Unterhose(n)	dee oonterhoaze(n)
panty liner	die Slipeinlage	dee shlip ain larger
paper	das Papier	dass papeer
paper (writing)	das Schreibpapier	dass shraip papeer
paprika	der Paprika	dayr papreeker
paraffin oil	das Petroleum	dass petrolayoom
parasol	der Sonnenschirm	dayr zonnensheerm
parcel	das Paket/das	dass pakayt/dass
	Päckchen	pekshen
pardon	die Entschuldigung/	dee entshool dee
	die Verzeihung	goong/dee
		fayrtsayoong
parents	die Eltern	dee elltern

park	der Park	dayr park
park (car)	parken/	parken/
	(Sw.) parkieren	parkeeren
parking space	der Parkplatz	dayr parkplats
parsley	die Petersilie	dee payterzeelier
part	das (Ersatz)teil	dass (ayrzats)tail
partition	die Trennwand	dee trennwant
partner	der Partner	dayr partner
party	das Fest/die Party	dass fest/dee party
passable	begehbar/(vehicle)	begaybar,
	befahrbar	befarbar
passenger	der Passagier	dayr passajeer
passport	der (Reise)pass	dayr (raizer)parss
passport photo	das Passbild	dass passbilt
patient	der Patient	dayr patseeyent
pavement	der Gehsteig/	dayr gayshtaik/
	das Trottoir	dass trottwar
pay	(be)zahlen	be)tsarlen
pay the bill	abrechnen	aprekhnen
peach	der Pfirsich	dayr pfeerzikh
peanuts	die Erdnüsse	dee ertnuesser
pear	die Birne	dee beerner
peas	die Erbsen	dee airpsen
pedal	das Pedal	dass pedarl
pedicure	die Fusspflege	dee fusspflayger
pen	der Stift	dayr shtift
pencil	der Bleistift	dayr blaishtift
penis	der Penis	dayr payniss
pension	die Pension	dee ponseeyoan
pepper	der Pfeffer	dayr pfeffer
performance	die Theatervorstel-	dee tayartter for
	lung	shtelloong
perfume	das Parfüm	dass parfuem
perm (to have a)	eine Dauerwelle	einer dowerveller
	machen	makhen
perm	die Dauerwelle	dee dowerveller
permit	die Genehmigung/	dee genay migoong/
	die Erlaubnis	dee erlowpniss
person	die Person	dee payrzoan
personal	persönlich	payrzoenlikh
petrol	das Benzin	dass bentseen
petrol station	die Tankstelle	dee tank shteller
pets	die Haustiere	dee howz teerer
pharmacy	die Apotheke	dee appotayker
phone (tele-)	das Telefon	dass talayfoan
phone	telefonieren	taylayfoaneeren
phone box	die Telefonzelle	dee taylayfoan tseller
phone directory	das Telefonbuch	dass taylayfoan bookh
phone number	die Telefonnummer	dee taylayfown noomer
photo	das Foto	dass foto
photocopier	das Kopiergerät	dass kopee gerayt
photocopy	fotokopieren	foto kopeeren
photocopy	die Fotokopie	dee fotokopee
pick up (an object)	aufheben	owfhayben
pick up	(ab)holen	(ap)hoalen
picnic	das Picknick	dass piknik

Word list 15

pier	die Landungsbrücke	*dee landoongz brueker*
pigeon	die Taube	*dee towber*
pill (contraceptive)	die Pille	*dee piller*
pill (morning-after)	die Pille danach	*dee piller danakh*
pillow	das Kissen	*dass kissen*
pillowcase	der Kissenüberzug	*dayr kissen ueber tsook*
pin	die Stecknadel	*dee shteknardel*
pineapple	die Ananas	*dee anarnass*
pipe	die Pfeife	*dee pfaifer*
pipe tobacco	der Pfeifentabak	*dayr pfaifen tarbak*
pity	schade	*sharder*
place of interest	die Sehenswürdigkeit	*dee zayenz vuerdeekh kait*
plan	der Plan	*dayr plarn*
plant	die Pflanze	*dee pflantser*
plasters	das (Heft)pflaster	*dass (heft)pflaster*
plastic	das Plastik	*dass plastik*
plastic bag	die Tüte	*dee tueter*
plate	der Teller	*dayr teller*
platform	das Gleis	*dass glais*
platform	der Bahnsteig	*dayr barnshtaik*
play (theatre)	das Theaterstück	*dass tayarter shtuek*
play	spielen	*shpeelen*
playground	der Spielplatz	*dayr shpeelplats*
playing cards	die Spielkarten	*dee shpeelkarten*
pleasant	angenehm	*angenaym*
please	bitte	*bitter*
pleasure	das Vergnügen	*dass fairgnuegen*
plum	die Pflaume	*dee pflowmer*
pocketknife	das Taschenmesser	*dass tashen messer*
point	zeigen	*tsaigen*
poison	das Gift	*dass gift*
police	die Polizei	*dee poleetsai*
police station	die Polizeiwache	*dee poleetsai vakher*
policeman	der Polizist	*dayr poleetsist*
pond	der Teich	*dayr taikh*
pony	das Pony	*dass poanee*
pop concert	das Popkonzert	*dass pop kontsert*
population	die Bevölkerung	*dee befoelke roong*
pork	das Schweinefleisch	*dass shvainerflaish*
port	der Port(wein)	*dayr port(vain)*
porter	der Pförtner	*dayr pfoertner*
porter	der Gepäckträger	*dayr gepek trayger*
post code	die Postleitzahl	*dee post lait tsarl*
post office	das Postamt	*dass postamt*
post office (main)	die Hauptpost	*dee howptpost*
postage	das Porto	*dass porto*
postbox	der Briefkasten	*dayr breef kasten*
postcard	die Ansichtskarte/die Postkarte	*dee ansikhts karter/ dee post karter*
postman	der Briefträger	*dayr breeftrayger*
potato	die Kartoffel	*dee kartoffell*
	(Aus.) die Heurigen	*dee hoyrigen*
poultry	das Geflügel	*dass gefluegel*

140

pound	das Pfund	*dass pfoont*
powdered milk	das Milchpulver	*dass milkhpulver*
power point	der Elektroanschluss	*dayr elektro anshluss*
pram	der Kinderwagen	*dayr kinder vargen*
prawns	die Garnelen	*dee garnaylen*
precious	lieb/teuer	*leep/toyer*
prefer	vorziehen	*fortseehen*
preference	die Vorliebe	*dee forleeber*
pregnant	schwanger/in	*shvanger/in anderen*
	anderen Umständen	*oomshtenden*
present	vorhanden/(person)	*forhanden/*
	anwesend	*anvayzent*
present	das Geschenk	*dass geshenk*
press	drücken	*druekken*
pressure	der Druck	*dayr drook*
price	der Preis	*dayr praiss*
price list	die Preisliste	*dee praisslister*
print	abziehen	*aptseehen*
print	der Abzug	*dayr aptsook*
probably	wahrscheinlich	*varshainlikh*
problem	das Problem	*dass problaym*
profession	der Beruf	*dayr beroof*
programme	das Programm	*dass programm*
pronounce	aussprechen	*owsshprekhen*
pub	die Kneipe	*dee knaiper*
pudding	der Pudding	*dayr pudding*
pull	ziehen	*tseehen*
pull a muscle	sich einen Muskel	*zikh ainen mooskel*
	verzerren	*fayrtserren*
pure	pur	*poor*
purple	lila	*leelar*
purse	der Geldbeutel	*dayr geltboytel*
purse	das Portemonnaie/die	*dass portmonnay/dee*
	Börse	*boerzer*
push	schieben/drücken	*sheeben/drueken*
puzzle	das Puzzle	*dass puzzle (pootsel)*
pyjamas	der Pyjama	*dayr peejarmar*

Q

quarter	das Viertel	*dass feartell*
quarter of an hour	die Viertelstunde	*dee fear tell shtoonder*
queen	die Königin	*dee koenigin*
question	die Frage	*dee frarger*
quick	schnell	*shnell*
quiet	ruhig	*roohikh*

R

radio	das Radio	*dass rardio*
railway	die (Bundes)bahn	*dee (boondez)barn*
rain	der Regen	*dayr raygen*
rain (verb)	regnen	*raygnen*
raincoat	der Regenmantel	*dayr raygenmantel*
raisins	die Rosinen	*dee rozeenen*
rape	die Vergewaltigung	*dee fair gevalti goong*
rapids	die Stromschnelle(n)	*dee shtroamshneller(n)*

rash	der Ausschlag	*dayr owsshlark*
raspberries	die Himbeeren	*dee himbeeren*
raw	roh	*roa*
raw vegetables	die Rohkost	*dee roakost*
razor blades	die Rasierklingen	*dee razeer klingen*
read	lesen	*layzen*
ready	fertig	*fairtikh*
really	eigentlich	*aigentlikh*
receipt (written)	der Empfangsschein	*dayr empfangs shain*
receipt (till-chit)	der Kassenzettel/die Quittung	*dayr kassentsettel/dee kvittoong*
recipe	das Rezept	*dass retsept*
reclining chair	der Liegestuhl	*dayr leegershtool*
recommend	empfehlen	*empfaylen*
recovery service	die Pannenhilfe	*dee pannen hilfer*
rectangle	das Rechteck	*dass rekhtekk*
red	rot	*roat*
red wine	der Rotwein	*dayr roatvain*
reduction	die Ermässigung	*dee ermayssigoong*
refrigerator	der Kühlschrank	*dayr kuelshrank*
region	die Gegend	*dee gaygent*
registration	der Kraftfahrzeug- schein	*dayr kraft far tsoyk shain*
relatives	die Verwandten	*dee fayrvanten*
reliable	zuverlässig	*tsoofayrlessikh*
religion	der Glaube(n)/die Religion	*dayr glowber(n)/die religioan*
rent out	vermieten	*fayrmeeten*
repair	reparieren	*repareeren*
repairs	die Reparatur	*dee reparatoor*
repeat	wiederholen	*veederhoalen*
report	die Anzeige	*dee antsaiger*
resent	übelnehmen	*uebel naymen*
reset	zurücksetzen	*tsooruek zetsen*
responsible	verantwortlich	*fayr antvort likh*
rest	ausruhen	*owsroohen*
restaurant	das Restaurant	*dass restorant*
result	das Ergebnis	*dass ergaypniss*
retired	pensioniert	*penzeeo neert*
return (ticket)	die Rückfahrkarte	*dee rueck far karter*
reverse (vehicle)	rückwärts fahren	*ruekverts faren*
rheumatism	das Rheuma	*dass roymar*
rice	der Reis	*dayr raiss*
ridiculous	unsinnig	*oonzinnikh*
riding (horseback)	das Reiten	*dass raiten*
riding school	die Reitschule	*dee raitshooler*
right	rechts	*rekhts*
right of way	die Vorfahrt	*dee forfart*
ripe	reif	*raif*
risk	das Risiko	*dass reezeeko*
river	der Fluss	*dayr flooss*
road	der Weg	*dayr vayk*
roadway	die Fahrbahn	*dee farbarn*
roasted	gebraten	*gebrarten*
rock	der Fels(en)	*dayr felz(en)*

Word list

roll	das Brötchen (S.Ger.,Aus.) die	dass broetshen
	Semmel,	dee zemmel,
	der Weck(en)	dayr vekk(en)
rolling tobacco	der Shag	dayr shag
roof rack	der Gepäckträger	dayr gepek trayger
room	das Zimmer	dass tsimmer
room number	die Zimmernummer	dee tsimmer noommer
room service	der Zimmerservice	dayr tsimmer zair viss
rope	das Seil	dass zail
rose	die Rose	dee roazer
rosé	rosa	roaza
roundabout	der Kreisverkehr/der	dayr krays fayr kayr/
	Kreisel/	dayr kraizel/
route	die Route	dee rooter
rowing boat	das Ruderboot	dass rooderboat
rubber	der/das Gummi	dayr/dass goommee
rubbish	der Quatsch	dayr kvatsh
rucksack	der Rucksack	dayr rookzak
rude	unhöflich	oonhoeflikh
ruins	die Ruinen	dee rooeenen
run (cross-country)	die Langlaufloipe	dee lang lowf loyper
run into	treffen	treffen

S

sad	traurig	trowrikh
safari	die Safari	dee zafaree
safe	sicher	zikher
safe	das Safe	dass sayf
safety pin	die Sicherheitsnadel	dee zikher haits nardel
sail	segeln	zaygeln
sailing boat	das Segelboot	dass zaygelboat
salad	der Salat	dayr zalart
salad oil	das Salatöl	dass zalartoel
salami	die Salami	dee zalarmee
sale	der Ausverkauf	dayr owsferkowf
salt	das Salz	dass zalts
same	der-/die-/dasselbe	dayr-/dee-/dasszelber
sandy beach	der Sandstrand	dayr zantshtrant
sanitary pad	die Damenbinde	dee darmen binder
sardines	die Sardinen	dee zardeenen
satisfied	zufrieden	tsoofreeden
Saturday	der Samstag/der	dayr zamstark/
	Sonnabend	zonnarbent
sauce	die Sosse	dee zoaser
sauna	die Sauna	dee zowner
sausage	die Wurst	dee voorst
savoury	herzhaft	hayrts haft
say	sagen	zargen
scarf	der Schal	dayr sharl
scenic walk	der Wanderweg	dayr vandervayk
school	die Schule	dee shooler
scissors	die Schere	dee sheerer
scooter	der Motorroller	dayr moatar roller
scorpion	der Skorpion	dayr skorpeeyoan
Scotland	Schottland	shottlant
Scotsman	der Schotte	dayr shotter

Word list

15

143

Scotswoman	die Schottin	*dee shottin*
Scottish	schottish	*shottish*
scrambled eggs	das Rührei	*dass ruehrai*
screw	die Schraube	*dee shrowber*
screwdriver	der Schraubenzieher	*shrowben tseeher*
sculpture	die Bildhauerei	*dee bilt hower rai*
sea	die See/das Meer	*dee zay/dass meer*
seasick	seekrank	*zaykrank*
seat	der Platz	*dayr plats*
seat	der Sitzplatz	*dayr zitsplats*
seat belt	der Gurt	*dayr goort*
seat reservation	die Platzkarte	*dee platskarter*
second	die Sekunde	*dee zekoonder*
second	zweite	*tsvaiter*
second-hand	gebraucht	*gebrowkht*
sedative	das Beruhigungs mittel	*dass berooee goongz mittel*
see (to)	sehen	*zayhen*
see (to) (view)	sich ansehen/besich tigen	*anzayhen/besikh tigen*
self-timer	der Selbstauslöser	*dayr zelpst ows loezer*
send	(ver)schicken	*(fair)shikken*
sentence	der Satz	*dayr zats*
September	der September	*dayr zeptember*
serious	ernst	*ayrnst*
service	die Bedienung	*dee bedeenoong*
serviette	die Serviette	*dee zairveeyeter*
sewing thread	das Nähgarn	*dass naygarn*
shade	der Schatten	*dayr shatten*
shallow	flach	*flakh*
shampoo	das Shampoo	*dass shampoo*
shark	der Hai	*dayr hai*
shave	rasieren	*razeeren*
shaver	der Rasierapparat	*dayr razeer apparart*
shaving brush	der Rasierpinsel	*dayr razeer pinzel*
shaving soap	die Rasierseife	*dee razeer zaifer*
sheet	das Laken	*dass larken*
sherry	der Sherry	*dayr sherry*
shirt	das (Ober)hemd	*dass (oaber)hemt*
shoe	der Schuh	*dayr shoo*
shoe polish	die Schuhcreme	*dee shookraymer*
shoe shop	das Schuhgeschäft	*dass shoogesheft*
shoemaker	der Schuhmacher/ Schuster	*dayr shoomakher/ shooster*
shoes (mountaineering)	die Bergschuhe	*dee bayrk shooer*
shop	einkaufen/einholen	*ainkowfen/ainhoalen*
shop	der Laden	*dayr larden*
shop assistant	die Verkäuferin	*dee fayrkoyferin*
shop window	das Schaufenster	*dass showfenster*
shopping centre	das Einkaufszentrum	*dass ainkowfs tsentroom*
short	kurz	*koorts*
short circuit	der Kurzschluss	*dayr koorts shlooss*
shorts	die kurze Hosen	*dee koortser hoazen*
shoulder	die Schulter	*dee shoolter*
show	die Show/die Schau	*dee shoa/dee show*

144

shower	die Dusche	dee doosher
shutter	der Auslöser	dayr owsloezer
side	die Seite	dee zaiter
sieve	das Sieb	dass zeep
sign	unterschreiben	oontershraiben
sign	das Schild	dass shilt
signature	die Unterschrift	dee oonter shrift
silence	die Stille	dee shtiller
silver	das Silber	dass zilber
silver-plated	versilbert	fayrzilbert
simple	einfach	ainfakh
single	unverheiratet/ledig	oonfayrhai-rartet/laydikh
single	der Junggeselle/die Junggesellin	dayr yoong gezeller/dee yoong gezellin
single	Einzel-	aintsel-
single (ticket)	einfach	ainfakh
sir	mein Herr	main hayr
sister	die Schwester	dee shvester
sit	sitzen	zitsen
sit down	sich setzen	zikh zetsen
size	die Grösse	dee groersser
ski	Ski fahren/laufen	sheefahren/lowfen
ski boots	Skischuhe	sheeshooer
ski goggles	die Skibrille	dee sheebriller
ski instructor	der Skilehrer	dayr sheelairer
ski lessons/class	die Skistunde(n)	dee sheeshtoonder(n)
ski lift	der Skilift	dayr sheelift
ski pants	die Skihose	dee sheehoazer
ski pass	der Skipass	dayr sheepass
ski slope	die Skipiste	dee sheepister
ski stick	der Skistock	dayr sheeshtok
ski suit	der Skianzug	dayr sheeantsook
ski wax	das Skiwachs	dass sheevakhs
skiing (cross-country)	der Langlauf	dayr langlowf
skimmed	halbfett	halpfett
skin	die Haut	dee howt
skirt	der Rock	dayr rock
skis	die Skier	dee sheeyer
skis (cross-country)	die Laufskier	dee lowf sheeyer
sleep	schlafen	shlarfen
sleeping car	der Schlafwagen	dayr shlarfvargen
sleeping pills	die Schlaftabletten	dee shlarf tabletten
slide	das Dia	dass deear
slip	der Unterrock	dayr oonterrock
slip road	die Auffahrt	dee owffahrt
slow	langsam	langzarm
slow train	der Nahverkehrszug	dayr narfayrkairs tsook
small	klein	klain
small change	das Wechselgeld	dass vekhselgelt
small change	das Kleingeld	dass klaingelt
smell	stinken	shtinken
smoke	der Rauch	dayr rowkh
smoke	rauchen	rowkhen
smoked	geräuchert	geroykhert
smoking compartment	das Raucherabteil	dass rowkher aptail
snake	die Schlange	dee shlanger
snorkel	der Schnorchel	dayr shnorkhel

snow (verb)	schneien	shnaien
snow	der Schnee	dayr shnay
snow chains	die Schneekette	dee shnayketter
soap	die Seife	dee zaifer
soap box	die Seifenschachtel	dee zaifen shakhtel
soap powder	das Seifenpulver	dass zaifen pullfer
soccer	der Fussball	dayr fussball
soccer match	das Fussballspiel	dass fussball shpeel
socket	die Steckdose	dee shtekdoazer
socks	die Socken	dee zokken
soft drink (lemonade)	die Limonade	dee limonarder
soft drink	das Erfrischungs-getränk	dass ayrfrishoongs getrenk
sole (fish)	die (See)zunge	dee (zay)tsoonger
sole	die Sohle	dee zoaler
solicitor	der Rechtsanwalt	dayr rekhts anvalt
someone	jemand	yaymant
sometimes	manchmal	manshmarl
somewhere	irgendwo	eergentvo
son	der Sohn	dayr zoan
soon	bald	barlt
sorbet	das Sorbet	dass sorbay
sore	das Geschwür	dass geshvuer
sore throat	die Halsschmerzen	dee halz shmayrtsen
sorry	Entschuldigung/ Verzeihung	entshool deegoong/ fayrtsayoong
sort	die Sorte	dee zorter
soup	die Suppe	dee zoopper
sour	sauer	zower
sour cream	der Sauerrahm	dayr zowerrarm
source	die Quelle	dee kveller
south	der Süden	dayr zueden
souvenir	das Andenken/das Souvenir	dass andenken/dass zooveneer
spaghetti	die Spaghetti	dee shpagetti
spanner (open-ended)	der Gabelschlüssel	dayr garbel shluessel
spanner	der Mutternschlüssel	dayr muttern shluesell
spare	die Reserve	dee rezayrver
spare parts	die Ersatzteile	dee erzats tailer
spare tyre	der Reservereifen	dayr rezayrver raifen
spare wheel	das Reserverad	dass rezayrverrart
speak	sprechen	shprekhen
special	besonders	bezonderz
specialist	der Spezialist/ der Facharzt	dayr shpetseealist/dayr fakhartst
speciality	die Spezialität	dee shpetseea lee tayt
speed limit	die Höchst-geschwindigkeit	dee hoekhst geshvindikh kait
spell	buchstabieren	bookh shtarbee ren
spicy	gewürzt	gewuertst
splinter	der Splitter	dayr shplitter
spoon	der Löffel	dayr loeffel
sport	der Sport	dayr shport
sports (to do)	Sport treiben	shport traiben
sports centre	die Sporthalle	dee shporthaller
spot	der Platz/Ort	dayr plats/dayr ort
sprain	verstauchen	fayrshtowkhen

spring	der Frühling	dayr fruehling
square	der Platz	dayr plats
square	quadratisch	kvadrartish
square metre	der/das Quadratmeter	dayr/dass kvadrart mayter
squash	das Squash	dass skvash
stadium	das Stadion	dass shtadeeon
stain	der Fleck	dayr flek
stain remover	das Fleckenmittel	dass flekken mittel
stairs	die Treppe	dee trepper
stalls	das Parkett	dass parkett
stamp	die Briefmarke	dee breefmarker
start	starten/anlassen	shtarten/anlassen
station	der Bahnhof	dayr barnhoaf
statue	das Standbild/das Denkmal	dass shtantbilt/dass denkmarl
stay (verb)	bleiben	blaiben
stay (verb)	wohnen	voanen
stay	der Aufenthalt	dayr owfenthalt
steal	stehlen	shtaylen
steel (stainless)	der (rostfreie) Stahl	dayr (rosstfraier) shtarl
stench	der Gestank	dayr geshtank
sting	stechen	shtekhen
stitch (med)	nähen	nayhen
stock	die Brühe	dee brueher
stockings	die Strümpfe	dee shtruempfer
stomach	der Magen/der Bauch	dayr margen/dayr bowkh
stomach ache	die Magenschmerzen/die Bauchschmerzen	dee margen shmayrtsen/dee bowkh shmayrtsen
stomach cramps	die Bauchkrämpfe	dee bowkh krempfer
stools	der Stuhl(gang)	dayr shtool(gang)
stop	halten	halten
stop	die Haltestelle	dee halter shteller
stopover	die Zwischenlandung	dee tsvishen landoong
storm	stürmen	shtuermen
storm	der Sturm	dayr shtoorm
straight (hair)	glatt(es Haar)	glatt(ez har)
straight ahead	geradeaus	gerarderows
straw	der Trinkhalm	dayr trinkhalm
strawberries	die Erdbeeren	dee ayrtbeeren
street	die Strasse	dee shtrarsser
street side	die Strassenseite	dee shtrarssen zaiter
strike	der Streik	dayr shtraik
study	studieren	shtoodeeren
subtitled	untertitelt	oonterteetelt
succeed	glücken	gluekken
sugar	der Zucker	dayr tsooker
suit	der Anzug	dayr antsook
suitcase	der Koffer	dayr koffer
summer	der Sommer	dayr zommer
summertime	die Sommerzeit	dee zommertsait
sun	die Sonne	dee zonner
sun hat	der Sonnenhut	dayr zonnenhoot
sunbathe	sich sonnen	zikh zonnen
Sunday	der Sonntag	dayr zonntark
sunglasses	die Sonnenbrille	dee zonnenbriller
sunrise	der Sonnenaufgang	dayr zonnen owf gang

147

sunset	der Sonnenuntergang	*dayr zonnen oonter gang*
sunstroke	der Sonnenstich	*dayr zonnenshtikh*
suntan lotion	die Sonnen(schutz)-creme	*dee zonnen(shoots) kraymer*
suntan oil	das Sonnen(schutz)öl	*dass zonnen(shoots)oel*
supermarket	der Supermarkt	*dayr zooper markt*
surcharge	der Zuschlag	*dayr tsooshlark*
surf	surfen	*zoorfen*
surf board	das Surfbrett	*dass zoorfbrett*
surgery	die Sprechstunde	*dee shprekh shtoonder*
surname	der Nachname	*dayr nakhnarmer*
surprise	die Überraschung	*dee ueber rashoong*
swallow	runterschlucken	*roonter shlooken*
swamp	der Sumpf	*dayr zoompf*
sweat	der Schweiss	*dayr shvaiss*
sweet (a)	das Bonbon	*dass bonbon*
sweet (nice)	lieb	*leep*
sweet (sugary)	süss	*zuess*
sweetcorn	der Mais	*dayr maiss*
sweetener	der Süßstoff	*dayr zuess shtoff*
sweets	Süssigkeiten	*zuessikh kaiten*
swim	schwimmen/baden	*shvimmen/bardern*
swimming pool	das Schwimmbad/ (spa)die Badeanstalt	*dass shvimmbart/ dee barder anshtalt*
swimming trunks	die Badehose	*dee barder hoazer*
swindle	der Betrug	*dayr betrook*
switch	der Schalter	*dayr shalter*
synagogue	die Synagoge	*dee zuena goager*

T

table	der Tisch	*dayr tish*
table tennis	das Tischtennis	*dass tishtennis*
tablet	die Tablette	*dee tabletter*
take	nehmen	*naymen*
take	dauern (time)	*dowern*
take pictures	fotografieren	*foto grafeerren*
talcum powder	der Talkpuder	*dass talkpooder*
talk	reden	*rayden*
tampons	die Tampons	*dee tampons*
tap	der (Wasser)hahn	*dayr (vasser)harn*
tap water	das Leitungswasser	*dass laitoongs vasser*
taste	probieren	*probeeren*
tax free shop	der Taxfree-Shop	*dayr taksfree-shop*
taxi	das Taxi	*dass tarksi*
taxi stand	der Taxistand	*dayr tarksishtant*
tea	der Tee	*dayr tay*
teapot	die Teekanne	*dee taykanner*
teaspoon	der Teelöffel	*dayr tay loeffell*
telegram	das Telegramm	*dass taylaygramm*
telephone (by)	telefonisch	*taylayfoanish*
telephoto lens	das Teleobjektiv	*dass taylay obyek teef*
television	der Fernseher	*dayr fayrnzayer*
telex	das Telex	*dass teleks*
temperature	die Temperatur	*dee temperatoor*
temporary filling	die Notfüllung	*dee noatfueloong*
tender	zart	*tsart*
tennis	das Tennis	*dass tennis*

Word list

15

tennis ball	der Tennisball	*dayr tennisbarl*
tennis court	der Tennisplatz	*dayr tennisplats*
tennis racket	der Tennisschläger	*dayr tennis shlayger*
tent	das Zelt	*dass tselt*
tent peg	der (Zelt)hering	*dayr (tselt)hayring*
terrace	die Terrasse	*dee terasser*
terribly	entsetzlich	*entzetslikh*
thank	danken, sich bedanken	*danken, zikh bedanken*
thank you	vielen Dank	*feelen dank*
thanks	vielen Dank	*feelen dank*
thaw	tauen	*towen*
the day after tomorrow	übermorgen	*ueber morgen*
theatre	das Theater	*dass tayarter*
theft	der Diebstahl	*dayr deepshtarl*
there	da/dort	*da/dort*
thermal bath	das Thermalbad	*dass termarlbart*
thermometer	das Thermometer	*dass termomayter*
thick	dick	*dik*
thief	der Dieb	*dayr deep*
thigh	der Oberschenkel	*dayr oaber shenkel*
thin	dünn/mager	*duenn/marger*
things	die Sachen	*dee zakhen*
think	denken	*denken*
third	das Drittel	*dass drittel*
thirst	der Durst	*dayr doorst*
this afternoon	heute nachmittag	*hoyter nakhmittark*
this evening	heute abend	*hoyter arbent*
this morning	heute morgen	*hoyter morgen*
thread	der Faden	*dayr farden*
thread	das Garn	*dass garn*
throat	die Kehle	*dee kayler*
throat lozenges	die Halstabletten	*dee hals tablet ten*
throw up	(sich) erbrechen	*(zikh) ayrbrekhen*
thunderstorm	das Gewitter	*dass gevitter*
Thursday	der Donnerstag	*dayr donnerstark*
ticket (admission)	die (Eintritts)karte	*dee (aintritts)karter*
ticket (travel)	die (Fahr)karte	*dee (far)karter*
ticket	das Ticket	*dass ticket*
tie	die Krawatte	*dee kravatter*
tights	die Strumpfhose	*dee shtroompf hoazer*
time	die Zeit	*dee tsait*
times	mal	*marl*
timetable	der Fahrplan	*dayr farplan*
tin	die Dose/die Büchse	*dee doazer/dee buekhser*
tip	das Trinkgeld	*dass trinkgelt*
tissues	Papiertaschentücher	*papeer tashen tuekher*
toast	das Toastbrot	*dass toastbroat*
tobacco	der Tabak	*dayr tabak*
tobacconist's	der Tabakladen	*dayr tabaklarden*
	(Aus.) die (Tabak) trafik	*dayr tabaklarden dee (tabak) trafeek*
toboggan	der Schlitten	*dayr shlitten*
today	heute	*hoyter*
toe	der Zeh/die Zehe	*dayr tsay/dee tsayer*
together	zusammen	*tsoozammen*

toilet	die Toilette	dee twarletter
toilet	das W.C.	dass vaytsay
toilet paper	das Toilettenpapier	dass twarletten papeer
toiletries	die Toilettenartikel	dee twarletten arteekel
tomato	die Tomate	dee tomarter
tomato purée	das Tomatenmark	dass tomarten mark
tomato sauce	der Tomatenketchup	dayr tomarten ketchup
tomorrow	morgen	morgen
tongue	die Zunge	dee tsoonger
tonic water	das Tonic	dass toanik
tonight	heute nacht	hoyter nakht
too much	zuviel	tsoofeel
tool	das Werkzeug	dass vayrktsoyk
tooth	der Zahn	dayr tsarn
toothache	die Zahnschmerzen	dee tsarnshmayrtsen
toothbrush	die Zahnbürste	dee tsarnbuerster
toothpaste	die Zahnpasta	dee tsarnpaster
toothpick	der Zahnstocher	dayr tsarnshtokher
top up	nachfüllen	nakhfuellen
total	total/insgesamt	totarl/insgezamt
tough	zäh	tsay
tour	die Rundreise	dee roontraizer
tour guide	der Reiseführer	dayr raizerfuerer
tourist card	die Touristenkarte	dee tooristen karter
tourist class	die Touristenklasse	dee tooristen klasser
Tourist Information Office	das Fremdenverkehrsbüro	dass fremden fayrkayrz buero
tourist menu	das Touristenmenü	dass tooristen menue
tow	(ab)schleppen	(ap)shleppen
tow cable	das (Ab)schleppseil	dass (ap)shlepzail
towel	das Handtuch	dass hanttookh
tower	der Turm	dayr toorm
town	die Stadt	dee shtatt
town hall	das Rathaus	dass rarthowz
town walk	der Stadtrundgang	dayr shtatroontgang
toy	das Spielzeug	dass shpeeltsoyk
traffic	der Verkehr	dayr fayrkayr
traffic light	die Verkehrsampel	dee fayrkayrs ampel
train	der Zug	dayr tsook
train ticket	die Fahr-/Bahnkarte	dee far-/barnkarter
train timetable	der Fahrplan	dayr farplarn
trainers	die Sportschuhe	dee shportshooer
translate	übersetzen	ueber zetsen
travel	reisen	raizen
travel agent	das Reisebüro	dass raizer buero
travel guide	der Reiseführer	dayr raizerfuerer
traveller	der/die Reisende	dayr/dee raizender
traveller's cheque	der Reisescheck	dayr raizershek
treacle/syrup	der Sirup	dayr zeeroop
treatment	die Behandlung	dee behandloong
triangle	das Dreieck	dass draiek
trim	kürzen	kuertsen
trip	der Ausflug/die Reise	dayr owsflook/dee raizer
trouble	die Beschwerde	dee beshverder
trout	die Forelle	dee foreller
trunk code	die Vorwahl	dee forvarl

try on	anprobieren	anprobeeren
tube (inner)	der Schlauch	dayr shlowkh
tube	die Tube	dee toober
Tuesday	der Dienstag	dayr deenstark
tumble drier	der Trockner	dayr trokner
tuna	der Thunfisch	dayr toonfish
tunnel	der Tunnel	dayr toonnel
turn	das Mal	dass marl
TV	das T.V./Fernsehen	dass tayfow/ fayrnzayhen
TV guide	die Rundfunk- und Fernsehzeitschrift	dee roont foonk- oont fayrn zay tsait shrift
tweezers	die Pinzette	dee pintsetter
tyre	der Reifen	dayr raifen
tyre lever	der Reifenheber	dayr raifen hayber
tyre pressure	die Reifenspannung	dee raifen shpannoong

U

ugly	hässlich	hesslik
umbrella	der Regenschirm	dayr raygensheerm
under	unten	oonten
underground	die U-Bahn	dee oo-barn
underground railway system	das U-Bahnnetz	dass oo-barnnets
underground station	die U-Bahnhaltestelle	dee oo-barn halter shteller
underpants	die Unterhose	dee oonterhoazer
understand	begreifen	begraifen
underwear	die Unterwäsche	dee oontervesher
undress	sich freimachen/(gen.) sich ausziehen	zikh fraimakhen/ zikh owstseehen
unemployed	arbeitslos	arbaitsloas
uneven	ungleichmässig	oon glaikh mayssig
university	die Universität	dee oonee vayrsee tayt
unleaded	bleifrei	blaifrai
up	nach oben	nakh oben
urgency	die Eile	dee ailer
urgent	dringend	dringent
urine	der Harn	dayr harn
usually	meistens	maistens

V

vacate	räumen	roymen
vaccinate	impfen	impfen
vagina	die Vagina	dee vageena
vaginal infection	die Scheidenentzündung	dee shaiden ent tsuen doong
valid	gültig	gueltik
valley	das Tal	dass tarl
valuable	wertvoll	vayrtfoll
van	der Lieferwagen	dayr leefer vargen
vanilla	die Vanille	dee vaniller
vase	die Vase	dee varzer
vaseline	die Vaseline	dee vasseleener
veal	das Kalbfleisch	dass kalpflaish
vegetable soup	die Gemüsesuppe	dee gemuezer zupper
vegetables	das Gemüse	dass gemuezer

Word list

15

vegetarian	der Vegetarier	*dayr vegetareeyar*
vein	die Ader	*dee arder*
venereal disease	die Geschlechtskrank-heit	*dee geshlekhts krank hait*
via	über	*ueber*
video recorder	der Videorecorder	*dayr video recorder*
video tape	das Videoband	*dass videobant*
view	die Aussicht	*dee owsikht*
village	das Dorf	*dass dorf*
visa	das Visum	*dass veezum*
visit (verb)	besuchen	*bezookhen*
visit	der Besuch	*dayr bezookh*
vitamin	das Vitamin	*dass vitameen*
vitamin tablets	Vitamintabletten	*vitameen tabletten*
volcano	der Vulkan	*dayr voolkarn*
volleyball	der Volleyball	*dayr volleyball*
vomit	sich erbrechen	*zikh erbrekhen*

W

wait	warten	*varten*
waiter	der Ober	*dayr oaber*
waiting room	das Wartezimmer	*dass varter tsimmer*
waitress	die Kellnerin/ die Serviererin	*dee kelnerin/ dee zayrveeererin*
wake up	wecken	*vekken*
Wales	Wales	*vaylz*
walk	der Spaziergang	*dayr shpatseer gang*
walk (verb)	spazierengehen	*shpatseeren gayhen*
wallet	die Brieftasche	*dee breeftasher*
wardrobe	der Kleiderschrank	*dayr klaider shrank*
warm	warm	*varm*
warn	warnen	*varnen*
warning	die Warnung	*dee varnoong*
warning triangle	das Warndreieck	*dass varn draieck*
wash	waschen	*vashen*
washing	die Wäsche	*dee vesher*
washing line	die Wäscheleine	*dee vesher lainer*
washing machine	die Waschmaschine	*dee vashmasheener*
washing-powder	das Waschmittel	*dass vashmittel*
wasp	die Wespe	*dee vesper*
water	das Wasser	*dass vasser*
water ski	das Wasserski	*dass vassershee*
waterproof	wasserdicht	*vasserdikht*
wave	die Welle	*dee veller*
wave-pool	das Wellenbad	*dass vellenbart*
way	die Weise	*dee vaizer*
way (path)	der Weg	*dayr vayk*
we	wir	*veer*
weak	schwach	*shvakh*
weather	das Wetter	*dass vetter*
weather forecast	der Wetterbericht	*dayr vetter berikht*
wedding	die Hochzeit	*dee hokhtsait*
Wednesday	der Mittwoch	*dayr mitvokh*
week	die Woche	*dee vokher*
weekend	das Wochenende	*dass vokhen ender*
weekend duty	der Notdienst	*dayr noatdeenst*
weekly ticket	die Wochenkarte	*dee vokhen karter*

welcome	willkommen	*villkommen*
well	gut	*goot*
west	der Westen	*dayr vesten*
wet	nass	*nass*
wetsuit	der Surfanzug	*dayr zoorfantsook*
what	was	*vass*
wheel	das Rad	*dass rart*
wheelchair	der Rollstuhl	*dayr rollshtool*
when	wann	*van*
where	wo	*vo*
which	welch-(-e,-er,-es)	*velkh-(-er,-er,-es)*
whipped cream	die Schlagsahne/ der Schlagrahm (Aus.) das Schlagobers	*dee shlarkzarner/ der shlarkrarm dass shlarkoberz*
white	weiss	*vaiss*
who	wer	*vayr*
wholemeal	das Vollkorn	*dass follkorn*
wholemeal bread	das Vollkornbrot	*dass follkornbroat*
why	warum	*vahroom*
widow	die Witwe	*dee vitveh*
widower	der Witwer	*dayr vitver*
wife	die Frau	*dee frow*
wind	der Wind	*dayr vint*
windbreak	der Windschutz	*dayr vintshoots*
windmill	die Windmühle	*dee vint mueler*
window	das Fenster	*dass fenster*
windscreen wiper	der Scheibenwischer	*dayr shaiben visher*
wine	der Wein	*dayr vain*
wine card	die Weinkarte	*dee vainkarter*
winter	der Winter	*dayr vinter*
witness	der Zeuge	*dayr tsoyger*
wonderful	herrlich	*hayrlikh*
wood	das Holz	*dass holts*
wool	die Wolle	*dee voller*
word	das Wort	*dass vort*
work	die Arbeit	*dee arbait*
working day	der Arbeits-/der Werktag	*dayr arbaits-/dayr vayrktark*
worn	abgenutzt	*apgenootst*
worried	beunruhigt	*be-oonroo-ikht*
wound	die Wunde	*dee vunder*
wrap (gift)	einpacken	*ainpakken*
wrist	das Handgelenk	*dass hantgelenk*
write	schreiben	*shraiben*
write down	aufschreiben	*owfshraiben*
written	schriftlich	*shriftlikh*
wrong	falsch/verkehrt	*falsh/fayrkayrt*

Y

yacht	die Yacht	*dee yakht*
year	das Jahr	*dass yahr*
yellow	gelb	*gelp*
yes	ja	*yar*
yesterday	gestern	*gestern*

Word list

15

yoghurt	der/(Aus.) das Joghurt	*dayr yoghoort*
you (polite)	Sie	*zee*
you too	gleichfalls	*glaikhfals*
youth hostel	die Jugendherberge	*dee yoogent hayr bayrger*

Z

zebra crossing	der Zebrastreifen	*dayr tsebra shtraifen*
zip	der Reissverschluss	*dayr raiss fayr shlooss*
zoo	der Zoo	*dayr tsoo*

Basic grammar

1 Nouns

German nouns are divided into three types, known as genders:
masculine, feminine, and neuter. German also has a system of cases
for its nouns, four in number, and referred to in English as Nominative
(for the subject), Accusative (for the object), Genitive (the possessive
case), and Dative (the *to* or *for* case).

2 Definite article (the)

	Masculine	Feminine	Neuter
Nominative	**der**	**die**	**das**
Accusative	**den**	**die**	**das**
Genitive	**des**	**der**	**des**
Dative	**dem**	**der**	**dem**

The plural is the same for all:

Nominative	**die**
Accusative	**die**
Genitive	**der**
Dative	**den**

3 Indefinite article (a or an)

	Masculine	Feminine	Neuter
Nominative	**ein**	**eine**	**ein**
Accusative	**einen**	**eine**	**ein**
Genitive	**eines**	**einer**	**eines**
Dative	**einem**	**einer**	**einem**

Note that when masculine and neuter nouns are in the possessive
(genitive) case, they have an s at the end, not totally unlike English; **der
Hund des Mannes** (the man's dog).

4 Plurals

Nouns can be rather erratic. There are a few basic principles:

Nouns ending in **-keit** and **-heit** and **-ung** add the letters **-en** to form
the plural.

Neuheit (novelties) becomes **Neuheiten** (novelties); **Sehenswürdigkeit**
(something worth seeing, tourist attraction) becomes
Sehenswürdigkeiten (tourist attractions); **Hoffnung** (hope) becomes
Hoffnungen (hopes). Also, as a general rule, if a word ends in an **-e**,
assume you can make the plural by adding an n; **Witwe** (widow)
becomes **Witwen** (widows).

In the case of masculine and neuter nouns making the plural not
infrequently involves making a change in the vowels within the word
as well as adding an ending. Try adding the sound **-e** or **er** to the
singular form, and you should be able to put the meaning across.

In the plural form of the Dative case, all nouns add an **-n**. **Berg**
(mountain) is a masculine noun (**der Berg**), and becomes **Berge** in the
plural (mountains); on the mountains becomes **auf den Bergen**.

5 Adjectives

Adjectives come in front of the noun. There is an arrangement for making the adjective agree with the noun if it is used without any article (no the or a), which is basically like **der, die, das**; Black thing, for example, is **schwarzes Ding**, pretty woman is **schöne Frau**, big dog is "**grosser Hund**".

If we place an article before the adjective, things are easier; the black thing is **das schwarze Ding**, the pretty woman is **die schöne Frau**, the big dog is **der grosse Hund**. Of the black thing; **des schwarzen Dings**. Of the pretty woman; **der schönen Frau**. Of the big dog; **des grossen Hunds**. (You may also hear **Dinges** and **Hundes**.)

6 Adverbs

Adverbs are essentially the same in German as adjectives; in other words, he does it well is **er tut es gut** (*err toot ez goot*), which means he does it good. Know one and you know the other.

7 Pronouns

	First (I)	Second (you)	Third (he)	(she)	(it)
Nominative	**ich**	**Sie**	**er**	**sie**	**es**
Accusative	**mich**	**Sie**	**ihn**	**sie**	**es**
Dative	**mir**	**Ihnen**	**ihm**	**ihr**	**ihm**

The forms for the plural, they, are **sie, sie, ihnen**.

Accordingly, he sees me becomes **er sieht mich**; she sees him: **sie sieht ihn**. I see it: **ich sehe es**.

The dative case is the case which occurs mostly if prepositions are involved (with, by, from, for example).

There is also a form for you which is used for close friends, talking to very small children, and animals; this is **Du**, and should be avoided unless you are really sure of your ground. There is a plural form of this, **ihr**.

The usual word for you is **Sie** (pronounced *zee*), and when written always has a capital letter for its forms, to distinguish it from the forms for they.

8 Verbs

German verbs, like English verbs, come in two kinds, traditionally referred to as strong and weak. Weak verbs are the regular ones, and are easy; strong verbs are irregular, and can really only be learnt. An example of a weak verb in English is to walk; I walk, I walked, I have walked. An example of a strong verb is to swim; I swim, I swam, I have swum.

The weak verbs make their forms which indicate action in the past in a regular way, too: I was loving is **ich liebte**; he was loving **er liebte**; we/you/they were loving: **Wir/Sie/sie liebten**. The strong verbs change the vowel in the main part of the verb: **ich schwimme** becomes **ich schwamm** (I swam).

A German weak verb looks like this:

Lieben,	To love
ich liebe	I love (also doubles up for I am loving, I do love)
(Du liebst)	(you love; this is the very friendly form)
er/sie/es liebt	he/she/it loves
wir lieben	we love
Sie lieben	you love
sie lieben	they love

The other difference between weak and strong verbs occurs in the past participle. Weak verbs are regular in their past participles; add the letters **ge-** to the front, and replace the **-en** at the end of the verb by a **-t**. **Lieben** (to love) gives us a past participle **gelebt** (loved); **spielen** (to play) gives **gespielt** (played), and so on.

Strong verbs do not make this change; e.g. **schwimmen** gives us **geschwommen** (**swum**), sehen (to see) gives us **gesehen**.

A quick look at the verbs "to have" and "to be":

Haben	To have
ich habe	I have
(Du hast)	(you have; very friendly form)
er/sie/es hat	he/she/it has
wir/Sie/sie haben	we/you/they have

Sein	To be
ich bin	I am
(Du bist)	(you are; very friendly form)
er/sie/es ist	he/she/it has
wir/Sie/sie sind	we/you/they are

In principle, the past form I have (done something) is created by using the relevant part of **haben** for verbs which have an object (I have seen him: **ich habe ihn gesehen**; I have done it: **ich habe es getan**), and the relevant parts of sein for verbs which do not have an object (I have swum: **ich bin geschwommen**; I have come: **ich bin gekommen**; I have flown: **Ich bin geflogen**). Bear in mind that, in the past form using have, the past participle comes at the end of the sentence.

9 Prepositions

in means in or into
auf means on or onto
mit means with
zu means to
for means for
bei means with or in the vicinity of (but rarely by)
von means of or from

Most prepositions are associated with the dative case, although some are found with the accusative e.g. **in der Stadt** : IN the town, **in die Stadt**: INTO the town.